SERIES EDITOR: LEE JOHNSON

OSPREY MILITARY MEN-AT-AR

GW00399993

ARGYLL AND SUTHERLAND HIGHLANDERS

TEXT BY
WILLIAM McELWEE

COLOUR PLATES BY
MICHAEL ROFFE

OSPREY
MILITARY

First published in Great Britain in 1972 by OSPREY, an imprint of
Reed Consumer Books, Michelin House, 81 Fulham Road, London SW3 6RB
Auckland and Melbourne

ISBN 0 85045 085 3

Filmset in Singapore by Pica Ltd
Printed through World Print Ltd., Hong Kong

Editor: Iain MacGregor
Cover Design: Mike Moule

For a catalogue of all books published by Osprey Military please write to:
Osprey Marketing, Reed Consumer Books, Michelin House,
81 Fulham Road, London SW3 6RB

The Origins of the Regiment

On 1 July 1881 Viscount Cardwell's wholesale reorganization of the British Army brought into existence Princess Louise's Argyll and Sutherland Highlanders: an amalgamation of the old 91st Argyllshire Highlanders with the 93rd Sutherland Highlanders. On the face of it this was an improbable and not very promising combination. The two counties were geographically as far apart as any two areas north of the Highland Line could well be. The histories of the two regiments were equally diverse and divergent. They had never served together in the same theatre of war. They drew their recruits from widely different sources so that, while the 91st had great difficulty in maintaining even a majority of Scots, let alone Highlanders, in their ranks, the 93rd were regarded as the most solidly Highland of all the regiments in the Highland Brigade. In fact, the only common factor between the two was an unbroken record of gallantry and efficiency. Yet, as every modern reader knows, the combination was a tremendous success. The new regiment quickly acquired a glory all its own, a pride and a sense of cohesion,

which have enabled it to mount a battle for survival unique in recent history.

The roots of both regiments go back far beyond their official incorporation into the British Army, and stem from the misery and impoverishment which beset the Highlands after the Battle of Culloden. For many different reasons a large reservoir of good fighting manpower suddenly became available to the Hanoverian government; and in addition to the regular regiments raised almost immediately for the Seven Years War, no less than twenty were raised from the Scottish Highlands between 1759 and 1793, thus contributing still further to that depopulation which remains

Duncan Campbell, 8th Lochnell, who raised the 91st for the Duke of Argyll, and was their first Colonel

an acute problem to this day. It was from some of these that the 91st, officially gazetted in February 1794 as the 98th Highlanders, and the 93rd, incorporated in 1799, took their origins.

The extreme Whig and anti-Stuart prejudices of the Campbell chieftains had brought into temporary being a Hanoverian regiment during the actual rebellion of '45; and there had been two Argyll Fencible regiments in 1759 and 1778. Colonel John Campbell of Barbreck in 1778 raised a second West Highland regiment which was called the Argyll Highlanders; but he had to fall back on a large number of recruits from Glasgow and the Lowlands, owing to the preference of 'the lower orders in Argyllshire' for naval rather than military service. All but four of his officers, however, were Highlanders, and twenty-three of them were Campbells. These too were disbanded at the end of the American war; and when the Duke of Argyll in 1793 was requested by George III to raise a local regiment, he had to start again more or less from scratch.

The Duke was in poor health when the King's letter reached him, and did not feel disposed to take any active part in the business beyond vetting the list of officers. He therefore deputed the task

Typical costumes of recruits on their way to Fort George to join the 93rd: mountain crofters, men from the prosperous farms of the coastal plains, and fisher folk

of raising an Argyllshire regiment to his kinsman, Duncan Campbell, 8th Lochnell, then a Captain in the 1st Foot Guards. Apart from some jockeying among the field officers and captains for seniority, the recruiting of officers presented few problems. The semi-feudal hold of the Clan was still powerful enough to obtain almost all that was needed locally; and when, some eighteen months later, the new regiment embarked for South Africa, 15 of the 33 officers were Campbells and 2 of the others had married Campbell ladies. Only in the matter of an adjutant – then a much less august figure in the military hierarchy than he has since become – were the Duke's ambitions foiled. He had set his heart on having a 'gentleman'; but Lochnell had in the end apologetically to accept a promoted ranker from the 79th.

But the required number of NCOs and rank and file simply could not be found in Argyllshire. Lochnell's personal tour of Lorne and the Isle of Mull had disappointing results; and when, on 15 April, he took over command of his new regiment, only about a third of the 689 rank and file were genuine Highlanders. The rest came largely from Glasgow and Edinburgh, Renfrew and Paisley, with a small contingent of Irish. This proportion, with a steadily increasing Irish element, was to remain typical of the 91st throughout its independent existence. The officers continued to be drawn mainly from Argyllshire, and there were always enough genuine Highlanders to give the regiment its characteristic stamp. Over the years the obstinate War Department preference for general service enlistment, and the rapid transfers resulting from the need to bring regiments abroad up to a higher establishment, added to the alien Irish large numbers of Englishmen who only slowly and reluctantly took to wearing the kilt. All were in the end successfully absorbed; and despite fifty years of entrenched official disapproval, the 91st maintained with equal obstinacy their Highland tradition. On 9 July 1794 they were formally gazetted into the British Army, but only, to Lochnell's fury, as the 98th Argyllshire Highlanders. The Duke's approved list of officers had been mislaid in Lord Amherst's office at the Horse Guards, and they had consequently lost four or five steps in seniority. It was not until four years later that, in October 1798, as a result of various disbandments, they were renumbered as the 91st.

The raising of the 93rd Sutherland Highlanders, in April 1799, was an even more feudal affair. In the remote and mountainous north, the semi-feudal, but essentially patriarchal, loyalties of the old clan organization still survived to a remarkable degree in the teeth of the English government's systematic attempt to destroy it. Sutherland and Caithness, and Lord Reay's Mackay country in the far north-west, suffered as heavily as any part of the Highlands from the evils of depopulation; and from their sparse numbers they had made an outstanding contribution to the military demands of King George III in his American difficulties. The 1st Sutherland Fencibles, raised by Lord Reay in 1759, had as little opportunity of military glory as any other home defence force of the period. But on disbandment in 1763 they had achieved the much rarer distinction that in a regiment of 1,050 men there had been no restrictions in four years and not one flogging.

The 2nd Sutherland Fencibles were raised in 1779 from the same background, nominally by Elizabeth, the thirteen-year-old heiress of the late Earl and a remarkably attractive character. 'I have no objection', she wrote to her uncle, 'to raising a Sutherland regiment; am only sorry I cannot command it myself.' In practice the task was delegated to her cousin, William Wemyss of Wemyss, a Coldstream subaltern aged nineteen, who was thus suddenly launched on a distinguished military career as a Temporary Lieutenant-Colonel; and in 1793, by then substantive in his rank, he raised the 3rd Fencibles, who were the direct ancestors of the 93rd. For, after serving in Ireland during the '98 rebellion, and emerging, almost unique, with a high reputation from that inglorious campaign, they returned to Fort George to be disbanded in April 1799, at the very moment when William Wemyss, now a Major-General and their titular Colonel, had been entrusted with the formation of a new regiment of Sutherland High-landers. He was thus able to take over five of the Fencible officers directly, and by 23 April he had already attested ninety-four non-commissioned officers and men of the disbanding Fencibles. Out of the 653 of all ranks assembled by him at Inverness on 25 August, 259 had served in the Sutherland Fencibles; and when they were put on

Major-General William Wemyss of Wemyss, who raised the 93rd for Elizabeth, Countess of Sutherland, wearing the uniform of the 2nd Sutherland Fencibles

an augmented establishment in 1803 they drew all the extra numbers they needed from the disbanding Reay Fencibles (nearly all Mackays), from the Rothesay and Caithness Fencibles and from the Scots Militia.

Most of the remainder were drawn from the Countess's tenantry by a process which, though highly elegant, amounted to a form of conscription. General Wemyss would assemble the available young men of each parish and would walk down the line carrying a large, silver-bound, horn snuff mull, with an attendant bearing a bottle of whisky. Each likely young man was invited to step forward and take snuff with the General and, having drunk his dram, was understood to have been attested without further formality. The only fierce objections came from the parents; and most

'Big Sam' – Sergeant Samuel Macdonald in the uniform of the 3rd Sutherland Fencibles, from which he transferred to the 93rd

Scottish regiments, and it remained so to the day in 1946 when it went into what the War Office called 'suspended animation'.

One individual deserves special mention in this context, since he was not only a remarkable person in himself, but was a living symbol of the close continuity of the 93rd with its Fencible predecessors. Sergeant Macdonald, born at Lairg in 1762, was six foot ten inches tall and measured forty-eight inches round the chest. After serving with the 2nd Sutherland Fencibles throughout their existence, he remained for a time in the army as fugleman in the Royal Scots. He was then porter to the Prince of Wales at Carlton Lodge, during which period he put in a brief appearance at Drury Lane as Hercules in *Cymon and Iphigenia*. In 1793 ancestral loyalty brought him back to the 3rd Sutherland Fencibles as a Sergeant in the Colonel's Company, where he had a special allowance of 2s. 6d. a day from the Countess of Sutherland, who took the view that 'so large a body must require more sustenance than his military pay could afford'. Like many immensely strong men, he was extremely gentle; and he was always accompanied on ceremonial parades by his pet red deer, also remarkable for its size. Along with the tallest of the Mackays, from the Reay Fencibles, who stood over six foot two, he paraded always on the right of the line in the 93rd, to avoid untidiness; and the two of them, along with the red deer, invariably led the newly formed regiment on the march 'to clear the way'. His gravestone, dated 9 May 1802, is in the Strangers' Cemetery at St Peter Port, Guernsey, and was last restored by the officers of the 93rd – the 2nd Battalion, The Argyll and Sutherland Highlanders – in 1927.

So the two regiments which later constituted the Argyll and Sutherland Highlanders came into being. The 98th, within two months of Lochnell taking over command at Stirling, were shipped via Leith to Southampton, still only half-drilled and very partially clothed, to spend an exacting winter at Netley under canvas and a pleasant summer in and around Chippenham, where they completed their training. They were required to bring their numbers up to active service establishment by local recruiting, and in the end succeeded very well, especially in Bristol. But they had to concede that all new recruits should be allowed

of these the Countess was able to reconcile by the grant of a more advantageous lease. At the finish Wemyss had 419 Highlanders, 91 of them named Mackay, 61 named Sutherland, and a further 200 with local clan names. But even these figures are misleading. For many years the Highland Line remained to the 93rd a remote and irrelevant geographical conception. 'Highlanders' meant the Gaelic-speaking mountaineers of their own country. Men from Caithness and the low-lying coastlands, and even those who came from Orkney and the Shetlands, were classed as Lowlanders, of whom there were, in all, 178. There were only three Englishmen, two of whom, however, had good Scots names; and in any case all three were discharged within two years as unfit for service. Right from the start the 93rd became the most solidly and characteristically Highland of all the to wear trews instead of kilts; and so the first inroad was made upon their Highland identity. On 5 May 1795 they embarked, 33 officers and 816 other ranks strong, for the four months' voyage to South Africa and their first active service – a somewhat mild baptism of fire at Wynberg. The 93rd Sutherland Highlanders were formally gazetted in October 1800, and were immediately dispatched from Fort George, via Aberdeen, to Guernsey.

The 91st Argyllshire Highlanders, 1795-1815

The 98th Highlanders arrived at Simonstown in September 1795, as part of a force some 4,500 strong under Sir Alured Clarke, an ambitious officer for whom the conquest of the Dutch colony at the Cape was the one great chance of achieving military renown. But the luck was all against him. His Second-in-Command had already forced a landing with the advance guard, and had driven the Dutch off their only tenable defensive position in front of Cape Town. When, after a cautious and leisurely disembarkation lasting no less than ten days, Sir Alured faced the now vastly outnumbered Dutch at Wynberg, they cheated him of his great victory by running away after one ragged volley which cost his army 1 seaman killed and 17 soldiers wounded, 4 of them from the 98th. He made the best of a bad job with a general order thanking his troops for 'their spirited exertions and cheerful perseverance through every hardship' in terms

which Wellington would have thought fulsome after a major victory. So the 98th had, technically, their baptism of fire, and settled down as the permanent garrison, to suffer for seven unhappy years really serious casualties from the insalubrious climate and the insanitary conditions in Cape Castle. They lost 11 dead in the first month; and they seldom had less than 100 sick in hospital.

Much worse, however, for morale was the order in December to adopt the standard uniform of the British Army in India. Lochnell had been at vast trouble to fit them all out with six yards each of the dark green Campbell tartan with the black stripe. For the rest they wore the full Highland dress: scarlet coats faced with yellow for both officers and men; black stocks, leather for rank and file, velvet for the officers; diced hose in red and white with scarlet garters, and Highland shoes with yellow or gold oval shoe-buckles. Lace with black and white cotton for NCOs and men, silver for officers; and officers' epaulettes, when worn, were also of silver lace. All ranks wore the regulation Highland feather bonnet, and officers wore their own hair, clubbed over the ears with red rosettes on each club, and the queue tied with a black bow. All this had now to be abandoned for garments no more suitable for hot climates than the kilt, and drearily undistinguished: white trousers with black half-gaiters, scarlet tunics and absurd round, black, felt hats, 'at least 6 inches high with a 4-inch brim', curled up at the sides, with a plume over the left ear, white for the grenadier company, green for the light company and black for battalion companies.

In this costume, deeply resented by all ranks, the 98th soldiered on as the Cape Town garrison. There was little excitement to be had in a city of 1,200 houses inhabited by 5,000 free folk, Dutch and Coloured, and 10,000 black slaves. Food was cheap. But widespread deforestation had made firewood extremely expensive and also deprived the officers of any decent shooting. They improved their lot, however, by fetching out a pack of foxhounds and hunting jackal, while the troops stagnated and went down in large numbers with various local diseases. There was a brief flutter of military activity when the Dutch attempted to recover their colony in 1796. But their Admiral, faced with overwhelming military force on land and blockaded

The evolution of the 93rd cross-belt plates:
(1) 3rd Sutherland Fencibles, 1793–99; (2) Reay or
Mackay Fencibles, 1794–1802; (3) Sutherland
Local Militia, 1808–16; (4) 93rd Sutherland
Highlanders, 1800–10

May 1803. They were much depleted in numbers, having been heavily milked in their last months at the Cape to bring the regiments destined for India up to full strength; and it took them more than a year to get back their full Highland dress. From 1804 onwards the men were issued with six yards of tartan every two years for the upkeep of their kilts. All ranks wore the Kilmarnock bonnet, cocked, for fatigues and minor parades, covering it with the feather bonnet for ceremonial occasions. The plaid became increasingly a purely ceremonial garment, and officers were forbidden the kilt as ball and dinner dress. To compensate, they were allowed gold epaulettes instead of silver.

All this helped to keep up morale for another five years of inactive soldiering, moving about southern England as part of the forces hopefully gathered to defeat Napoleon if the admirals ever let him slip across the Channel. They had a brief hope of better things when the Highland Brigade was sent to Hanover at the end of 1805. But they were back in Kent throughout 1806, and thereafter in Cork. Throughout all this they clearly remained a very good regiment. They were ceaselessly inspected and invariably earned the 'Strong Approbation' of the generals. The Commander-in-Chief, H.R.H. the Duke of York, was 'Highly Pleased' with them in 1805. Rather more significantly, Sir John Moore was 'Extremely Well Pleased'; and before they left Dublin, in June 1808, to join Sir Arthur Wellesley's army in Portugal, they paraded for the Lord Lieutenant and gave him 'Great Satisfaction'.

Nevertheless, the campaign was as disappointing for the 91st as it was for the nation as a whole. The light company of the 91st was engaged at Roliça and had a sergeant severely wounded. But the regiment as a whole was in reserve and was not engaged in either of the major battles. It was again in the reserve division for Sir John Moore's spectacular march to Salamanca which disrupted Napoleon's whole campaign; and it came into its own at last when the reserve division became the rearguard for the epic retreat which culminated in Moore's victory and death at Corunna. The 91st had then more than their fair share of privations and forced marches; and in the rearguard actions in which they were engaged they lost 164 of all ranks killed, wounded or missing. At Corunna

by a superior fleet at sea, surrendered without landing a man or firing a shot. Sir James Craig followed Clarke's example by issuing some grandiose general orders, particularly thanking Lieutenant McNab and twenty mounted men of the 98th who had picketed the coast while he marshalled his forces. The grenadier and light companies had a little excitement with a Boer farmer rebellion in 1799; and the light company had some experience of warfare with Africans inland from Algoa Bay in 1800. Morale in the regiment was never allowed seriously to sink. With a typical Scots desire for self-improvement they formed a regimental school, with a fee of 1s. a month; and from Scotland Lochnell busied himself with the formation of a regimental band.

Thus, nothing very decisive had happened to the now renumbered 91st when, under the terms of the Treaty of Amiens, they handed Cape Colony back to the Dutch and reassembled at Bexhill in

A rather feeble depiction of the Light Company of the 93rd Sutherland Highlanders landing at the Cape of Good Hope – but it shows good details of parts of the uniform

The devastating low fever peculiar to the island of Walcheren had already destroyed one British army 200 years before. This time, from 3 September to 23 December, an army of 40,000 men lay encamped there because the generals could not agree on what to do with them. During these four months no less than 35,000 of them passed through the military hospitals to a precarious convalescence or the grave. By 25 September, after only three weeks, the 91st had only 246 rank and file fit for duty out of 608. From disease the regiment lost a total of 218 dead – far more than all their casualties in the Corunna campaign. During the six months following their return to Kent they had an average of 250 sick, and it was quite impossible to train or drill them to any acceptable standard. On top of this they were deprived of even their trews and bonnets. Henceforth they wore the blue-grey trousers and black cap of an English line regiment: a uniform in which few of the troops and none of the officers took the smallest pride. All that remained of their origin was the Pipe Band and the title of His Majesty's 91st Argyllshire Regiment.

As such, they rejoined Wellington in 1812. They missed Vitoria. But with the 6th Division at Sorauren on 28 and 30 July 1813, in what Wellington called 'bludgeon work', they played a decisive part in dislodging Marshal Soult from the positions he had hoped to hold in the Pyrenees. On the first day the 91st suffered heavily, losing 115 killed and wounded out of a total strength of 821. On the second day, when the brigaded light companies bore the brunt, they got off lightly. But they clearly played their full part in what even Wellington called 'desperate fighting', adding that he had 'never known the troops behave so well'. 'Pyrenees' was another battle honour on the 91st Colours which was well and truly earned. They were to win four more in France: 'Nivelle', 'Nive', 'Orthes', 'Toulouse', with 'Peninsula' thrown in as a general makeweight. The first three were not costly, and the only distinction was the promotion in the field of the Adjutant, Lieutenant MacNeil of Colonsay – Lochnell had at last got a 'gentleman' – after he had had two horses killed under him at the passage of the Nivelle.

At Toulouse, on 10 April 1814, Soult put up a last, desperate fight, which cost Wellington close

itself, though 'in the very centre of the line and next the Guards', they were not heavily engaged and lost only two men wounded. 'Corunna', nevertheless, was a worthily won battle honour to be placed on the Colours beside 'Roliça' and 'Vimeiro'.

But for the 91st the rest of the year 1809 was disastrous. The first and, from the point of view of regimental morale, the worse blow was the loss of their kilt and of their status as a Highland regiment. It was, of course, from the office of the Adjutant-General, whose clerks have for over 200 years put their own convenience before the interests of the fighting soldier, that the blow fell. Recruiting difficulties and the allegation that their national dress was 'objectionable to the natives of South Britain' were made the excuse for striking six regiments off the Highland establishment, though in fact the 91st enlisted in all, between 1800 and 1818, 970 Scots as against 171 Englishmen, 218 Irishmen and 22 foreigners, mostly Germans. Moreover from 1807 to 1814 their 2nd Battalion recruited 599 Scots, 168 Englishmen, 142 Irishmen and 197 foreigners. Since the tartan had already been issued for new kilts, the 91st found some consolation in having it made up into trews; and they adopted a flat, black bonnet ornamented with a single feather. This was the uniform in which they were dispatched on what the history books always call the 'ill-fated' Walcheren expedition.

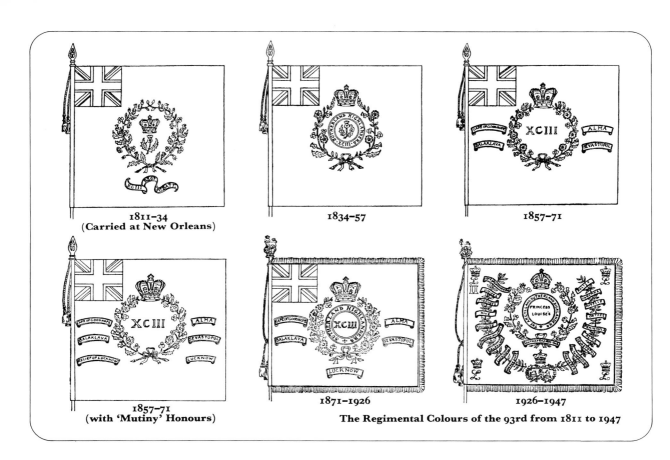

1811–34
(Carried at New Orleans)

1834–57

1857–71

1857–71
(with 'Mutiny' Honours)

1871–1926

1926–1947

The Regimental Colours of the 93rd from 1811 to 1947

on 5,000 casualties. Sir Denis Pack's Highland Brigade led the 6th Division attack brilliantly, ending up with the 42nd and 78th holding three captured enemy redoubts, and the 91st in close support in a farmyard behind. The crunch came when a French column, 6,000 strong, counter-attacked. The 42nd were driven back in some disorder, but the prompt support of the 91st gave them time to re-form; and the two battalions together then successfully restored the position. By the time the 91st got back to their farmhouse the other wing was in trouble; once more they sallied out, again completely restored the position and incidentally rescued a large party of the 78th who had been surrounded and were in danger of being made prisoner. Every general present reckoned that only the prompt and vigorous support afforded by the Argyllshire regiment had saved the Brigade at a very critical moment in the battle. So the war ended for the 91st in a blaze of glory, with nine battle honours on the Regimental Colour. But at Waterloo they were left far on the right flank; and though they got the campaign medal, that great battle was never inscribed on their Colours. One more fragment of military glory nevertheless came their way. The 2nd Battalion, raised purely as a feeder for the 1st, was a pretty motley crew. At their annual inspection in 1809 the older men were still wearing out their forbidden kilts, the rest were wearing 'pantaloons, breeches, or trews', and they could only muster 130 all ranks. But their acquisition three years later of a dynamic Commanding Officer, Lieutenant-Colonel Ottley, some able lieutenants and 309 disbanded militiamen, encouraged the War Department to bring them up to full strength with all sorts of 'undesirables' – 'old, worn-out men', 'an inferior type of boy' and some displaced Swedes, Pomeranians and Hanoverians – and send them to the Baltic. They saw their first and last action at the disastrous night attack on the fortress of Bergen-op-Zoom in 1814, and thanks to Ottley's training did very well. All four of the assaulting columns successfully stormed the outer walls, only to be thrown back by superior numbers of veteran French troops manning the inner defences. The

Battalion withdrew in admirable order, leaving 13 officers and an unrecorded number of men wounded, and losing altogether 45 killed or mortally wounded. So far as is known, the Surgeon and Assistant Surgeon were the only unwounded to fall into enemy hands; and Sergeant-Major Cahill was commissioned in the field for saving the Regimental Colour when the ensign carrying it went down. So, having unexpectedly found a niche in military history, the 2nd Battalion came home to be disbanded after sending 240 men to the 1st Battalion for the Waterloo campaign.

The 93rd Sutherland Highlanders, 1800-1815

Unlike the 91st, the 93rd had from 1800 to 1815 a relatively stable and peaceful existence. They were brought back from Guernsey after two years and in February 1803 they were sent to quell a brief recrudescence of rebellion in Dublin. In this difficult role, all too familiar to British soldiers, they managed to become quite popular with the Irish and yet keep them in order. Their recipe was 'kind and steady, yet decided conduct', and seems to have worked everywhere as they moved about Ireland for the next three years. They spent one fortnight aboard ship under orders, fortunately cancelled, for Jamaica. Instead they sailed, in July 1805, to recapture Cape Colony; there, like the 91st, they had their baptism of fire and won their first – for many years their only – battle honour.

The Dutch were better prepared this time.

General Janssen had nearly 2,000 regular infantry, a squadron of dragoons, and 16 guns served by a mixed crew of Europeans, Javanese and black slaves from Mozambique. He had hoped for a substantial reinforcement of mounted burghers, but the harvest kept all but 224 at home. Major-General Sir David Baird had on his transports three times Janssen's numbers; but he had to get them and their guns ashore on open beaches through a heavy surf and prevent their dying from thirst and heat-exhaustion on the inevitably long approach march. His first attempted landing, on 5 January 1806, was foiled by the surf, and he therefore sent an infantry regiment and his cavalry to secure a comparatively easy landing miles away, in case he should have to take the whole force round and accept the appalling administrative problem of supplying it for several days in a waterless desert before he could make contact with his enemy. Actually he got his force ashore the next day for the loss of only 37 of the 93rd, all of whom were still cheering madly as their boat turned over. More seriously, all the supplies and rations for the first day were lost, and for three days the army depended for water and everything else on what the navy could float in casks through the surf and then drag up over the soft, sandy soil. As Baird handsomely acknowledged in his dispatch, the army owed its survival entirely to the selfless toil of the seamen.

Janssen's tactic of holding back behind the Blauwberg Hills in the hope that the two-day approach march would at least partially destroy his enemy was thus very nearly justified; and he

A field kitchen of the 93rd in South Africa in 1807. White shell jackets and Kilmarnock bonnets were worn as fatigue dress

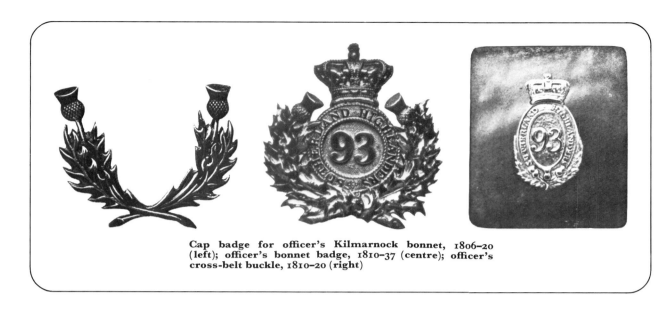

Cap badge for officer's Kilmarnock bonnet, 1806–20 (left); officer's bonnet badge, 1810–37 (centre); officer's cross-belt buckle, 1810–20 (right)

made a good fight of it. Baird made the odds nearly even by detaching a whole brigade to hold off what turned out to be only a handful of mounted burghers on his flank. He thus had only half his available force, his Highland Brigade, to face the whole Dutch Army; and on the field, infantry and guns were pretty evenly matched. The Highlanders fought without subtlety, merely deploying into line and, after a preliminary discharge of artillery, advancing with fixed bayonets and the pipers in front, pausing to fire one volley at extreme range, and then charging home. With the 93rd, young, enthusiastic and wholly inexperienced, in the centre of the line, it was probably the best way. Two-thirds of the 5th Waldeck Regiment left the field when the guns opened, though Janssen himself knocked the major in command down and shot one fugitive with his pistol. His rage inspired the rest of his troops to make a stout fight of it; and when he drew off in good order he left 400 killed and wounded and had inflicted some 200 casualties on the Scots. The 93rd lost 5 officers wounded and 2 men killed; but 42 out of their 53 wounded died of their wounds.

This virtually ended the campaign. Cape Town was surrendered; and 7 of the disgraced Waldeck officers and 20 of their troopers committed suicide. Janssen tried himself to hold out for ten days in the mountains, finally surrendering his remaining 1,050 men, and with them Cape Colony, on 18 January. The surviving Waldeckers cheerfully accepted 20 dollars each to join the British Army; and the 93rd moved into the old home of the 91st in Cape Castle, where they remained for eight uneventful years.

They were thus given time and tranquillity to form that distinctive regimental character which set them a little apart even from the rest of the Highland Brigade, and which they would never quite lose as long as the regiment existed. It sprang initially, of course, from the close territorial connection of nearly all the officers and men. They even grouped together in the companies all the men from any one parish, so that any man who distinguished himself, for good or ill, was liable to find his name posted in the porch of his parish church to the pride or shame of his family. Moreover, almost all came from households where morning and evening prayers and Bible reading were an integral part of family life. Almost every private had his own Bible; and the later reputation of these men for steadfast endurance undoubtedly sprang from the deeply rooted religious habit established in their early years. Yet it was noted in Plymouth, when they returned to England in 1814, that 'their religious tenets were free of all fanatical gloom', and that 'they always promoted that social cheerfulness characteristic of the homes from which they came'. Later, when heavy casualties brought in recruits from less happy backgrounds, almost all were absorbed into the regimental tradition. Forty years later, in Canada, every man still carried his Bible and psalm book under his arm on church parade, and no less than 700 of them took Communion.

The effects of all this were already visible in Cape Town. A private's pay, after deductions, left him 1s. 7½d. a week spending money. But, with only a little help from the officers and better-paid NCOs, they subscribed a stipend for a Church of Scotland chaplain, built and equipped their own church, with 2 sergeants, 2 corporals, and 2 privates as elders, and even added their own very beautiful silver Communion plate. Many of them sent home substantial sums for the relief of poor relations; and they also managed handsome subscriptions to general charities. In their last eighteen months at the Cape they collected £1,400 'for books, societies, and the support of the Gospel'. While waiting on the transports for transhipment to England, they contributed £78 for the Gaelic School Society; and during their month in Plymouth they sent large sums north – one bank in Plymouth handled no less than £500 – for the relief of their families, evicted and ruined by Highland 'clearances'. They had of course all received an excellent elementary education in the parish church schools which the third Lord Reay had begun to found in the Mackay country before 1748, and which the SPCK had made available to almost every Highland parish by the end of the century. The men of the 93rd were thus enabled to earn considerable sums as part-time teachers in the Cape Town schools to supplement their pay. All in all, it was a very remarkable, cheerful and united body of men, much given to Highland dancing, which set sail in 1814 to take part in the British government's latest folly: an attempt to capture New Orleans.

For this expedition, for the only time in their history, the 93rd were deprived of their kilts and feathered bonnets and sent into action in tartan trews and a particularly unbecoming form of cocked Kilmarnock bonnet. But they were well led, and their morale was by now indestructible. This was just as well. For, as Private Neil McIntosh wrote home afterwards, 'General Mismanagement' commanded throughout. The admirals, whose greed for prize-money is said to have prompted the whole expedition, were callous and incompetent. The Commander-in-Chief, Sir

The Communion plate bought by subscription for the Regimental Church of the 93rd at Cape Town

Edward Pakenham, a good divisional commander, was helpless without Wellington's guidance; and his three brigade commanders were timorous and indecisive. None of the staff knew his job; and the result, for both troops and seamen, was three weeks of humiliating martyrdom.

The 93rd landed on the evening of 23 December, having spent, like the rest of the brigade, six days and nights packed in open boats, with inadequate rations, and exposed to continuous rain, sleet and a bitter north wind; and they moved up through the swamp to be involved piecemeal in a chaotic dog-fight which lasted all night. The advance guard had been surprised by a night attack by 1,200 hastily assembled militiamen; by dawn superior discipline and training prevailed, and the Americans withdrew, leaving behind 74 prisoners; and there the brigade stayed, nine miles from New Orleans, while the whole army, of some 6,600 men, came up into a position on the north bank of the Mississippi, where it was continuously galled by gunfire from two armed schooners out in the river. Pakenham came up on Christmas Day and for once took decisive action, destroying one schooner with red-hot shot and chasing the other off upstream. From then on he merely dithered.

General Andrew Jackson made his stand behind a canal some five miles forward of New Orleans. His right flank rested on the river; his left on a swamp. Across his mile-long front he built, out of cotton bales and sugar casks filled with earth, a

The New Orleans Battle, 8 January 1815, just before the débâcle. Light troops can be seen storming the enemy redoubt on the river bank. Both wings are still advancing, and the 93rd are moving up in company columns to form line in the centre

parapet twenty feet deep with a short glacis sloping down to the canal bank; and on it he mounted four well-protected heavy guns. Across the river he placed a battery covered by 1,500 militiamen, to enfilade the whole area in front of his main position, with the surviving schooner in midstream to thicken up its fire. Along his parapet, invisible and almost invulnerable, he had about 3,500 men. Pakenham's general advance on 28 December was brought to a halt some 750 yards in front of this position; and there, under bombardment, rain and sleet, the troops lay for five hours, while Pakenham conferred with his senior sapper, Colonel Burgoyne. They concluded that the position was not to be taken by a frontal assault, and the troops were withdrawn two miles into another makeshift bivouac after a miserable day during which they had lost 56 men to the Americans' 34. The 93rd's contribution was 2 killed and 5 wounded.

Another futile advance on 1 January, after a three-day bombardment of the American cotton bales, ended the same way, and cost the 93rd 1 officer and 9 men killed, and 10 men wounded. Undeterred, Pakenham ordered a third, and this time disastrous, assault on 8 January. Everything conceivable went wrong. The gun batteries could not be built because there was not enough earth.

Only a quarter of the force which was to storm the battery on the far bank and turn its guns on the enemy could be got across. Worst of all, Lieutenant-Colonel Moleyns, whose 44th Regiment were to carry up the fascines and scaling ladders for the assault on the right, forgot them. The total result was for the army a disgrace, and for the 93rd a tragedy.

On the right Moleyns lost his head and led the 44th in a panic flight which spread to the rest of Major-General Samuel Gibbs's Brigade. A few gallant parties crossed ditch and glacis without fascines or ladders, only to see the enemy in full flight in front and their own supporting troops in flight behind them. Gibbs was killed; and Pakenham, mistakenly riding into the chaos to stop the rot, was twice wounded and then also killed. On the left three light companies, among them the 93rd, stormed a redoubt on the river bank from which the whole enemy line could have been turned. But there too the Brigade Commander was killed, and the advance came to a standstill. The 93rd alone, pushed out into the centre of the battlefield by the confusion on their left, doggedly continued their advance until they were halted by a staff officer only 100 yards short of the ditch. Their Commanding Officer was killed. His successor, an officer who worked strictly by the book, would neither advance nor retire without a clear order. So there they stood rock-like, in close order, being slowly destroyed by the concentrated fire of the whole American line, until Lambert, the surviving General, after a careful survey, at last withdrew them. They came back with parade-ground precision, leaving three-quarters of their total strength killed or wounded, and having laid the foundations of an immortal legend: a reputation for disciplined and indomitable courage which was to last as long as the regiment. The British had nearly 2,000 casualties that day, of whom 557 were from the 93rd. The Americans behind their parapet had 6 killed and 7 wounded.

The 91st Argyllshire Regiment, 1815-1881

The basket hilt of Lieutenant G. Drummond's broadsword, 93rd Highlanders, 1826

For forty years after Waterloo a great lethargy settled upon the world's armies. Russia and Turkey had the excitement of a major war in 1828. For the rest, the monotony of garrison duty was only occasionally interrupted by street fighting against the 'Revolution' or minor colonial campaigns. Both were exhausting, sometimes dangerous, but rarely glamorous. For the British Army most of the fun and adventure was to be had by outlying companies and detachments on the frontiers of an expanding Empire.

For the 91st, 1815–81 was a particularly dreary period. After three years at Valenciennes as part of the Army of Occupation they had a spell in Ireland, followed by nine years in the destructive climate of Jamaica, made even more lethal by a perpetual ration of salt beef washed down with cheap rum. 'We were aye drinking, and we were aye thirsty', one man wrote afterwards. Yellow fever reduced their numbers at one time to less than 300; and, on average, 70 men and officers died each year. In 1826 they got new Colours to replace the tattered, hand-painted Peninsula Colours which still hang in St Giles's Cathedral in Edinburgh; and on their return they made, in

1832, a little history by travelling to Liverpool, on their way back to Ireland, on the first recorded troop train. Otherwise there is little to chronicle.

In 1836 they were given another miserable posting, to St Helena, where the only amusements were horse-racing and cockfights. This swallowed six more years of their regimental life, enlivened only by the mounting of a ceremonial guard over the remarkably well preserved remains of the Emperor Napoleon when they were removed, to be reinterred in Paris with appropriate pomp. Their reward from the French government was a large bronze medal for officers and men. But by the time they received it, Regimental Head-quarters and an advance party were already back in Cape Town where, after the passing of nearly three years, they were rejoined by the rest of the regiment. Meanwhile commanding officers and colonels never ceased to clamour for the return of the kilt and of their Highland identity, tenuously

Piper Angus Munro of the Light Company, the 93rd, with his wife or sweetheart; a contemporary drawing c. 1825

preserved by their Pipe Band and the designation 'Argyllshire' in the Army List. In 1842 their depot companies were, however, formed into a 2nd Battalion, which also joined them in South Africa, wearing the standard uniform of British line in-fantry, quite unsuited to hot climates, and for the 91st extremely damaging to morale.

The value of the acquisition of Cape Colony is not today easy to assess. In the middle years of the last century it certainly seemed a very poor bar-gain, involving endless troubles with rebellious Boer farmers, with African tribes, especially, later and more formidably, with Zulus. This meant that companies were constantly detached as parts of punitive or protective columns, or split up into even smaller groups in isolated outposts, guarding Afrikaner farmers against raids by Africans, or African tribes against Afrikaner reprisals. The strain on the 91st was particularly severe, as they had for once a thoroughly bad commanding officer who antagonized his officers and neglected his men. Long, hot, hard marches alternated with months of static boredom, both on often short and quite unsuitable rations. Only once was the batta-lion, as such, in action, and even then it only mustered 254 men. This was at Fort Peddie in 1846, during the War of the Axe, so called because it all started with two Africans stealing a hatchet during a peace conference; 8,000 Africans were beaten off and 200 casualties inflicted without the loss of a single man.

The Reserve Battalion had a much happier time. It landed in a blaze of glory on the night of 27 August 1842, when the troopship *Abercrombie Robinson* dragged her anchors in a gale and went on the rocks in Table Bay. All the senior officers had gone ashore on duty leave, and Captain Bertie Gordon, left in command, preserved such impec-cable control and discipline that, with only one serviceable lifeboat, he put ashore without loss 43 women, 63 children and all his 492 troops. Wellington, having received the official report, wrote that he had 'never read anything so satis-factory', and used his influence to get Regimental Sergeant-Major Murphy appointed a Tower Warder. Bertie Gordon was awarded a special pension of £100 a year and went on to become one of the best Commanding Officers the 91st ever had. Having lost all its kit, the Battalion was kept

A contemporary drawing of the band and pipers of the
93rd Sutherland Highlanders in the funeral procession of
the Duke of Wellington, 18 November 1852

in garrison at the Castle until the War of the Axe, in which it did very well; and it stayed behind when the 1st Battalion sailed for home in January 1848.

It arrived at Portsmouth in very poor shape. All young soldiers had been posted to the Reserve Battalion before sailing, and many of the seniors had taken their discharge and settled down in South Africa. The Battalion was only 360 strong, with not one man from Argyllshire and less than 70 Scots. At Gosport in that summer they had the only bad inspection report in their history; and at Dover in 1850 the Adjutant-General in person dealt the final blow to their morale by abolishing the bagpipes, the last link, as one officer sadly wrote home, with their regimental origin.

This was the lowest ebb in the fortunes of the 91st. The reserve battalion soldiered on in South Africa, fought creditably in the Second Kaffir War of 1851–3, and returned home to be disbanded into a number of depot companies stationed at Preston. The 1st went via Ireland to Malta and during 1855–8, once again well out of the lime-light, formed part of the Anglo-French garrison of Greece and the Ionian Islands. Its Crimean War casualties amounted to 190 men dead from accident or disease and the Paymaster, whose Greek house collapsed on top of him in the night. It then had the minor distinction of being the first British regiment to pass through the Suez Canal, but reached India too late for the Mutiny fighting, to fetch up at Kamptee, 'the fifth furnace of the world'. It was at that point that Bertie Gordon came out to take command, and the revival of the regiment began.

Gordon found Kamptee, in his own words, 'the most barbarous, the most inaccessible, the most neglected and the most forgotten station in British India', and transformed it into one of the happiest. Gordon, a typical Scotsman, was both a progressive thinker far ahead of his time and a traditionalist. He transformed the dreary Regimental Institute of Kamptee into a 'Soldiers' Coffee-Room, Reading-Room and Shop' of which a modern NAAFI might be proud. Everything was for sale that 'an officer, soldier, or soldier's wife could want'. There was a small kitchen, a branch post office, a spacious games room and a flower and vegetable garden. Six dusty acres were turned into soldiers' flower gardens where once a week, under lamplight, took place 'Colonel Gordon's Cremorne'. All ranks and their wives and children attended. There was a dancing floor and two bandstands in which the band and the pipers, privately maintained by officers' subscriptions, played alternately. Recreation apart, there were

17

The Doctor, the Chaplain, and the Major of the 1st Argyll Highland Rifle Volunteers in the 1880s

competitive exams for corporals and lance-corporals, and half their promotions were based on these instead of time-honoured seniority.

After four years of the less lively Indian stations, Gordon brought the 91st home in 1863, to resume the battle, bitterly fought by every colonel of the regiment since 1809, for the restoration of its Highland status. Brilliantly he exploited the powerful influence then exercised at Court by the Duke of Argyll to get the Queen to overrule the War Office. He could not get back the kilt, because that would have cost per man an extra 1s. a year. But the 91st was restored as a non-kilted Highland corps: 'Tunic as worn in all Highland regiments. Trews of the Campbell tartan. Chaco, blue cloth with diced band and black braid. Forage cap, Kilmarnock, with diced band. The officers to wear plaids and claymores': so ran the War Office order. But Scotland being Scotland, there followed a prolonged and acrimonious dispute as to the proper tartan to be restored to the regiment. All were agreed that the basis must be the old, dark green Campbell tartan, and that it must be the one worn by the 91st when it was first raised. Lochnell's original letter clearly laying down a black stripe had been mislaid. The Duke wanted the white line worn by his own Campbell branch. There was a strongly supported legend that the original had the red line of Lord Breadalbane and

the Cawdor Campbells; and Bertie Gordon wanted to design a quite new one with both red and white. In the end the red-liners won, and until 1881 the purists were to protest at the anomaly of a west coast regiment wearing an east coast tartan. The only sensible observation in the whole voluminous and somewhat ridiculous correspondence came from the Duke: 'The whole subject of tartans', he wrote, 'has got into hopeless confusion; if indeed (which I doubt) it was ever anything else but a very uncertain and varying custom.' But he strongly resented the final solution, since the red line was also worn by his hereditary enemies, the Atholls.

Once started, the process of Scottish rehabilitation proceeded apace. The next Colonel, John Sprot, adroitly petitioned for the privilege of finding the Guard of Honour for the wedding of H.R.H. Princess Louise to Argyll's son, the Marquess of Lorne. He marched them into Windsor Castle to the tune of 'Bonnie Mary of Argyll' and so pleased the Queen that she granted the 91st a perpetual right to march past behind their pipers; in 1872 they became 'Princess Louise's Argyllshire Highlanders', with her coronet and cipher and the Argyll Boar's Head and motto of 'Ne Obliviscaris' added to their insignia. Their depot moved to Stirling, and the regiment went to Inverness for its first Scottish tour of duty in eighty years.

So well were the 91st now dug in that during their three years at Inverness they furnished the Queen's Guard at Balmoral every summer. Then, after a spell in Ireland, they were back in South Africa for the Zulu War of 1879. Never was the importance of proper precautions, especially for all-round defence in savage warfare, better demonstrated than in Lord Chelmsford's campaign of that year. At Isandhlwana two whole regiments were virtually annihilated because they had formed no proper lager and were outflanked and infiltrated. When Chelmsford's own column was attacked by 10,000 Zulus at Ginginhlovo it had formed square. On the rear face the 91st met the brunt of the attack and broke it in twenty minutes, slaughtering 500 Zulus for the loss of only 1 man killed and 8 wounded. That was the last of their active service as an independent regiment; and to mark it they were granted on 1 June 1881, just before they were amalgamated with the 93rd, a final battle honour for their Colours, 'South Africa', to commemorate their three periods of campaigning in that country. They then became the 1st Battalion of the Argyll and Sutherland Highlanders.

The 93rd Sutherland Highlanders, 1815-1881

The withdrawal from New Orleans was as ill-managed as all the rest had been, and involved for the 93rd a two-day wait without any rations whatever until the boats got back from ferrying a first load of wounded and the two West Indian regiments who were dying from cold and exposure. Unabashed by all their disasters, General Lambert and Admiral the Hon. Sir Arthur Cochrane buoyantly set about planning a similar attempt on the town of Mobile. Fortunately for the troops and seamen, they were frustrated by the signature of preliminaries of peace. The wounded prisoners, all of whom had been admirably treated in American hospitals, were returned; and the 93rd were able to muster half their original strength when they landed at Spithead. They were helped back to full strength by a large draft from an ephemeral 2nd Battalion raised in 1815 and after a brief visit to Newfoundland disbanded at the end of that year. By 1823, having spent eight years in Ireland, the 93rd was back to its old form. There were only ten Englishmen and forty Irish; and Gaelic was still the native language of the rank and file.

Their service during the long peace conformed to the general pattern. They had a spell in Barbados, where the natives thought that their kilts were a penance imposed by George IV who, for some delinquency, was believed to have confiscated their breeches. Under the influence of that climate many of them drank too much rum. But their crime rate remained remarkably low. The Duke of Wellington was delighted with them when he presented new Colours to them on their return in 1834. Then they were in Canada for ten years, dealing with various local troubles and insurrections in that emergent nation; and in 1854 they were back in England, when the outbreak of hostilities with Russia brought them for the first time into the thick of things in a major theatre of war. They passed through Malta, spent the summer of 1854 on the unhealthy Black Sea coast of Bulgaria, where they were lucky enough to have only 54 men die of cholera, and by September were in the Crimea, making up with the 42nd and the 79th that Highland Brigade which, under Sir Colin Campbell, was to make much history.

The stories of the Highland Brigade at the Alma

Bandboys of the 93rd in 1856

A drill parade of the 93rd, Chobham Camp, 1854. The officers wear the short white hackle of the Grenadier Company, the NCOs the red and white of Battalion Companies. The piper, in drill order, wears a Kilmarnock bonnet with a cock's feather

and of the 93rd at Balaklava have been often told, yet will always bear retelling. The Alma, like all the Crimean battles, was essentially 'a soldiers' battle'. The Allied Army, marching south along the Crimean coast towards Sevastopol, found the Russians strongly established along and behind the heights on the far bank of the River Alma. Marshal Saint-Arnaud, in supreme command, had only his experience as a brigade commander in Algeria and in the street fighting in Paris which had put the Emperor Napoleon III on the throne, to guide him in the conduct of an army. Perhaps prudently, as Wellington said of Napoleon at Waterloo, 'he did not manœuvre at all'. He merely deployed his force and launched it in a frontal assault across the river. He had formed no clear idea of the enemy position, so that the French Army debouched on the right into a void only thinly held by the Russians. It was left almost entirely to the British to storm the crest from which the enemy batteries dominated the entire valley and then to carry the redoubts on the plateau beyond, where the Russians had concentrated their main strength. Lord Raglan could only order a general advance across the river and trust to the fighting quality of British infantry to see him through.

It was the Highland Brigade and the Guards on the British left who really covered themselves with glory on that day. With the Light Division skirmishing in front, they waded waist-deep through the river under heavy artillery fire, fought their way up to the crest, and there re-formed for the irresistible assault on the Russian redoubts which

decided the battle. The Highlanders had the good fortune to be commanded by one of the greatest military leaders of all time. Before he deployed them Sir Colin Campbell delivered a severely admonitory address, bidding them not to chatter, to hold their fire until they were ordered, and then to fire low. Wounded were to be left for the bandsmen to pick up; and if any soldier was seen to escort a wounded comrade off the field 'his name shall be stuck up in his parish porch'. 'Now, men,' he ended, 'the Army will watch us. Make me proud of the Highland Brigade.' He led them up the hill himself and, though his horse was shot under him, was with them on the crest to check their disorderly charge and have the line properly dressed for the final decisive advance. The Russians too had fixed bayonets and were prepared to charge; but the sight of the bare knees and the towering feathered bonnets emerging from the smoke so unnerved them that they prudently fell back.

Colin Campbell had all the showmanlike tricks as well as the courage of the born leader. Immediately after the battle he again addressed his brigade and told them that he was so pleased with them that he had obtained Lord Raglan's permission to wear a Highland bonnet instead of his general's cocked hat for the rest of the campaign. He was there and then formally presented with one, with a special hackle, the top third red for the 42nd, and the rest white for the 79th and the 93rd; and the cheer the men sent up was heard along the whole British line. He was to show the same qualities of leadership a month later at Balaklava, when the 42nd and 79th were up in the trenches before Sevastopol and he had only the 93rd and two Turkish battalions to protect the base on which the whole army depended for its supplies.

The Russian force engaged in the attack that day was 25,000 strong; but only their massed cavalry pushed right forward down the road to Balaklava. Part of this threat was parried by the immortal charge of Scarlett's Heavy Cavalry Brigade. The rest, a formidable mass, swept on to charge Sir Colin's mixed brigade which alone stood between them and the British base. The Turks on either flank fired one ineffectual volley at a range of 800 yards and bolted, leaving only the 93rd astride the road, drawn up in line, two

'The Thin Red Line', from the painting by Robert Gibb

deep. 'There is no retreat from here, men,' Campbell told them as he rode down the line. 'You must die where you stand.' And the reply of John Scott, the right-hand man, was taken up by them all: 'Ay, Sir Colin. An needs be, we'll do that.' They fired one volley, at 500 yards, from their new Minié rifles, which appeared to empty few saddles, and another, almost equally disappointing, at 250 yards. But at the second the cavalry mass split in half, swerving away at the gallop to right and left, and finally into full retreat. Some of the younger soldiers started excitedly forward for a bayonet charge, but once again the voice of Sir Colin rang out in admonition. '93rd, 93rd,' he called out in an unforgettable phrase, 'damn all that eagerness.'

The Russian withdrawal was not, in fact, merely a failure of nerve, for the new rifle had done better than the soldiers realized. Russian officers present said later that there was hardly a man in the charge who was not either hit himself or had his horse hit under him. But, as they pointed out, a wounded horseman will cling to his mount for as long as possible in the hope of being carried out of the battle, and a wounded horse will go on until it drops. So it was a genuine victory, worthy of the perpetual commemoration conferred on it initially by *The Times* correspondent, W. H. Russell, who, standing on the hills above with Raglan's anxious and excited staff, could clearly see that nothing stood between the Russian cavalry mass and the defenceless base but 'the thin red streak tipped with a line of steel' of the 93rd. Condensed almost

immediately into 'The Thin Red Line', the phrase has survived to this day as the chosen symbol of everything for which the Argyll and Sutherland Highlanders believe themselves to stand. But the last word was, as might be expected, spoken by Sir Colin Campbell when a daring staff officer asked him why he had been so unorthodox as to receive a cavalry charge in line instead of in square. 'I knew the 93rd,' he answered, 'and I did not think it worth the trouble of forming square.'

For the rest of the war the 93rd's history was that of any other Crimean regiment: a story of almost unendurable hardships from cold and maladministration stoically endured, until public outcry at home, largely stimulated by Mr Russell, at last forced the War Department to mend its ways. They were not heavily involved either at Inkerman, or in the two disastrous assaults on the Redan; and as the war petered slowly out, in May 1856, Sir Colin delivered a moving farewell address to the Highland Brigade, his 'brave soldiers', and 'kind comrades', before going home, as he thought, to retirement. The 93rd followed him a month later, expecting for their part a well-earned restful spell, preferably in Scotland.

Neither expectation was fulfilled. A year later the s.s. *Mauritius*, carrying 1,070 of the 93rd, 994 of them still genuine Scots, berthed at Calcutta, and the new Commander-in-Chief in India, sent out to deal with the crisis of the Mutiny, immediately came on board to welcome them, to be greeted with rapturous cheers as they recognized their beloved Sir Colin. The affection was mutual.

The 93rd embarking in the great steamship *Himalaya* for the Crimean War on 1 March 1854

Though a Black Watch man, Sir Colin seems always to have had a particular affection for the Sutherland Highlanders. When he set off on his desperate venture to relieve Lucknow with only 4,000 men, to meet four times that number of well-trained and desperate mutineers who had no choice but to win or die, the Governor-General wrote to cheer him on his way. 'You have', Lord Canning reminded him, 'your beloved 93rd.'

The campaign, a miniature masterpiece, reached its crisis on 11 November 1857, when the army, having fought its way up through Cawnpore and Lucknow's outer defences, faced the two great fortresses of the Sikanderbargh Gate and, behind it, the Shah Najaf, both solidly built, strongly manned, and heavily gunned. When his own gunners had knocked a hole no more than three feet square in the Sikanderbargh wall, Sir Colin ordered a drummer of the 93rd to sound the advance, and the regiment swept forward to the tune of 'The Haughs of Crondell' which had piped Montrose's Highlanders to so many victories for King Charles I. Nine officers and men got through the hole, including Colonel Ewart, in command, and the fourteen-year-old drummer boy, who was killed. Fighting fiercely hand-to-hand, and helped by a gallant assault from outside by some of the loyal 4th Punjabis, they got the gate open, and the 93rd cleared the fortress with a ferocity born of the horrors they had seen at Cawnpore.

There remained the still more formidable Shah Najaf; and as evening fell Sir Colin delivered another of his characteristic addresses to the 93rd: 'Soldiers,' he said, 'I had no intention of employ-ing you again today, but the Shah Najaf must be taken this evening. The artillery cannot drive the enemy out, so you must, with the bayonet, and I will lead you myself.' And so, for the last time in history, a Commander-in-Chief rode, sword in hand, among the pipers at the head of his leading infantry. They fought all night and lost a great number of men. But at dawn Sir Colin was able to order them to uncase their tattered Colours and fly them from the tower to show the hard-pressed defenders of the Residency that relief was at hand. This provoked a furious burst of fire from the enemy; and the epic ended with a twelve-year-old drummer who was with the Colour party defiantly playing 'Cock o' the North' on his pipes. In those twenty-four hours the 93rd won seven Victoria Crosses, a record only surpassed when the Lancashire Fusiliers won 'eight before breakfast' at Gallipoli.

To the eternal credit of Sir Colin and his troops, 1,000 wounded, 600 women and children, the King of Oudh with his household and treasure, £250,000 of government money and all the remaining stores, were brought out of the Residency without a shot being fired at them. After all that, the fierce fighting which still remained before the Mutiny was finally stamped out came as something of an anticlimax. Even then the 93rd had still ten years of Indian soldiering before they at last got back, in 1870, to their native Scotland. There they happily stayed until 1879, when they were sent for two years to Gibraltar; and then, in 1881, came the amalgamation with the 91st. It was to be a very happy and successful union. But the old 93rd, as Sir Colin knew them, ceased to exist.

The Argyll and Sutherland Highlanders, 1881-1918

The Cardwell reforms, intelligently conceived though they were, inevitably imposed some friction and hardships, and demanded immense patience and tolerance from the more junior regiments in the Army List which had only one battalion each and had perforce to amalgamate. In a country like Scotland, where details of tradition, custom and dress mattered more profoundly than any Englishman will ever understand, the strains and difficulties were unavoidably greater; and it was not always easy at first for the 91st and 93rd to work out an equitable compromise.

The 93rd suffered the worse and more irremediable loss. The general territorial regrouping gave Sutherland to the Seaforths as their recruiting area. The counties allotted to the Argyll and Sutherland Highlanders were Argyllshire, Stirling, Clackmannan, Dumbarton, Renfrew and Kinross. Only Argyll could furnish authentic Highlanders; and there had never been enough of them to outnumber the Lowlanders in the single battalion of the 91st. As the years went on, the new regiment was to depend increasingly on Glasgow for its recruits, many of them Irish; and but for its kilt and its very powerful, deeply rooted traditions it would have become indistinguishable from any

regiment in the Lowland Brigade. There would be no more marching to church with Bibles under the arm, and no more posting of names in parish churches. In the new regimental title only the word 'Sutherland' commemorated the old 93rd. They became Princess Louise's Argyll and Sutherland Highlanders, and as the years went on this was to mean much more than a merely formal attachment to the Royal Family. The Princess took a close and constant interest in the doings of her regiment which they repaid not just with respect, but with a very real affection. She designed the new regimental badge herself, elegantly combining the Argyll Boar's Head and the Sutherland Wild Cat, surmounted where suitable by her own cipher and coronet; and the motto of the new regiment was the old 91st 'Ne obliviscaris'.

In the matter of uniform, however, it was the 93rd who prevailed, which was probably just as well in view of the recent difficulties of the 91st. The Sutherland tartan was practically indistinguishable from the original 'dark green Campbell tartan with the black line' in which Lochnell had first raised the 91st. So the anomalous tartan with the red stripe disappeared. The new badger head sporran with its six white tassels and the feathered bonnet both derived essentially from the 93rd. The Kilmarnock bonnet, however, disappeared, and for the future all ranks wore the glengarry whenever they were in trews, for less formal parades, and in place of a forage cap. For the rest there were few problems, since Dress Regulations had always imposed a certain uniformity even on Highland regiments.

The 91st on manœuvres, 1894. An unfinished sketch by Lady Butler, clearly depicting the discomforts of formal dress in wet weather

'Over the Veldt', a contemporary drawing of the Pipes and Drums of the 91st in Zululand, 1884

Once these ticklish questions had been settled, the two regiments quickly settled down together as a singularly harmonious body. For seniority and promotion they were a single regiment, and all ranks happily accepted the continuous cross-postings, since they merely found themselves among a fresh set of old friends. Despite their miscellaneous origins the Argylls easily established themselves as a genuine entity in the Highland Brigade, partly perhaps because so many of the old names constantly reappear, generation by generation, among the officers, and the sons and grandsons of many famous figures in the old regimental histories continue to serve in whatever remnant successive cuts have left in being. But paradoxically, for all the cross-postings and interchangeability, each battalion mysteriously inherited and preserved the distinctive qualities of the old 91st and 93rd. They invariably referred to themselves by the old names; and in spite of their successful fusion, senior regulars of all ranks down to the end of the Second World War belonged and owed a special loyalty to the 91st or the 93rd, wherever they might be serving. The origins and backgrounds of the soldiers changed, but they were quickly absorbed into the military habits and traditions of the old regiments, which were too deeply rooted to be superseded. In action or out of it, the 1st Battalion remained always and recognizably the 91st, and the 2nd displayed un-mistakably the peculiar spirit and qualities of the 93rd.

Curiously, even the histories of the two battalions often showed the same characteristics as those of their ancestors. After its brief and glorious incursion into the main stream of military history, the 2nd Battalion – the 93rd – was for ten years the home-service battalion. It acquired a notable athletic reputation and for a spell had the honour of replacing the Scots Guards, absent on active service in Egypt, as the Queen's Guard at Windsor Castle. It then spent sixteen years in India, enhancing its reputation for sport but gaining no military laurels. It suffered all the discomforts of extreme heat and cold in the Tochi Field Force in Waziristan in 1897, and invented a special uniform

The pipe band of the 93rd in 1914, pipe-major on the left

1 **Officer, Battalion Company, 93rd Highlanders, 1801**
2 **Private, Battalion Company, 93rd Highlanders, 1805**
3 **Captain, 91st Argyllshire Highlanders, 1808**

MICHAEL ROFFE

A

1 Officer, Battalion Company,
  93rd Highlanders, 1834
2 Field Officer, 91st Argyllshire
  Highlanders, 1808
3 Sergeant, Grenadier Company,
  93rd Highlanders, 1814

B

MICHAEL ROFFE

1 Corporal, Grenadier Company,
  93rd Highlanders, 1838
2 Private, 91st Argyllshire Regiment, 1846
3 Piper, 93rd Highlanders, 1853

MICHAEL ROFFE

C

1 Officer, Light Company, 93rd
  Highlanders, 1853
2 Bandboy, 93rd Highlanders, 1856
3 Officer, 91st Highlanders, 1857

D

MICHAEL ROFFE

1 **Officer, Grenadier Company, 93rd Highlanders, 1857**
2 **Ensign, 93rd Highlanders, 1857**
3 **Lieutenant, 8th Argyll Rifle Volunteers, 1866**

MICHAEL ROFFE

E

1 Sergeant, 91st Highlanders,
  1874
2 Field Officer, Argyll and
  Sutherland Highlanders, 1882
3 Sergeant, Argyll and
  Sutherland Highlanders, 1882

F

1 Officer, Undress, Argyll and Sutherland Highlanders, 1892
2 Private, Volunteer Battalion, Argyll and Sutherland Highlanders, 1902
3 Private, Highland Division, 1940

MICHAEL ROFFE

G

1 Piper, Argyll and Sutherland Highlanders, 1960
2 Officer, Service Dress, Argyll and Sutherland Highlanders, 1960
3 Sergeant, Argyll and Sutherland Highlanders, 1965

H

for the occasion. But it was not engaged. Two unexciting years in South Africa followed; and from 1909 to 1914 it was back in Scotland preparing to form part of the Expeditionary Force promised to the French in the event of a German invasion of Belgium.

Similarly the 91st, as so often before, were almost continuously involved in the confusions of South African history. By 1884 they were back in Zululand in an exhausting, but not dangerous campaign. They kept their kilts this time, and took their pipes and drums with them, though they discarded their feathered bonnets in favour of a Cape felt hat, variously worn, but always decorated with a white hackle. They also adopted what was to be standard field wear for Highland units, a thin khaki apron to protect their kilts, with a large pocket in front to replace the sporran. They had three years in Ceylon and four in Hong Kong, and were scarcely back in Dublin when, in 1899, they were again warned for service in South Africa in what was to develop into the Boer War.

This time they were to be involved, for the first time since Toulouse, in the thick of the heaviest fighting, though with much less happy results. The Highland Brigade in the army with which Lord Methuen was attempting to relieve Kimberley was commanded by Colonel Wauchope, late of the Black Watch. The tactical conceptions of both commanders had been formed in forty years of peaceful manœuvres on Salisbury Plain and made no allowance for the mobility, fieldcraft, marksmanship and general wiliness of Boer farmers; and their troops paid a heavy penalty. Light-heartedly assuming that the bridge over the Modder River was undefended, Methuen got his whole force pinned down under devastatingly accurate fire from concealed positions on the far bank. Thanks to two intrepid subalterns, who waded the river waist-deep and formed a hand-to-hand chain behind them, the whole of the 91st did get across. There, unsupported, and again pinned down in some oak scrub on the far bank, they lay all day under a cruel sun which scorched the backs of their knees. Their rations had gone astray the day before and their water-bottles were empty. At nightfall, after a day of acute misery, they were withdrawn, having lost 30 killed and 92 wounded with nothing whatever to show for it.

The Tochi Field Force uniform, improvised for the Waziristan campaign of 1897

Two views of life in the Armentières trenches, 1914–15

25

There followed two similar tragedies. In their defence of the rocky, 4,000-foot-high Magersfontein kopje the Boers cheated on Lord Methuen's rules and cunningly entrenched themselves low down on the forward slopes. After an all-day bombardment of the empty summit the British infantry were launched in a night advance up the hill to carry the crest with the bayonet, only to run into an elaborate system of trip wires attached to flares which illuminated the whole battlefield and brought down a devastating fire. Wauchope, advancing in a close order which would have done him credit at Waterloo, was killed. His brigade, surprised, unled and confused by contradictory orders, broke in confusion and was only saved from total disgrace by the courage of Corporal Piper Jimmy Mackay of the Argylls standing immovable in the confusion playing 'The Campbells

Warrant and non-commissioned officers of the 2nd Battalion Argyll and Sutherland Highlanders at Aldershot in 1890. Left to right: Drum-major, pipe-major, sergeant, sergeant-major

Officer's belt buckle of the amalgamated Argyll Highlanders and Sutherland Highlanders, 1882. Designed by Princess Louise, this, shorn of the coronet and inscriptions, remains the collar badge of the regiment today

are Coming' until other pipers struck up along the line and the troops recovered their nerve. So, once again, they lay at point-blank range from the enemy under a devastating sun and without food or water until 2.00 p.m. the next day, when Methuen at last threw in his hand. But Lord Roberts, V.C., the hero of the nation, did little better for the Highland Brigade at Paardeberg Drift three months later. By sheer numbers he won the decisive victory of the war. But he sent the Highlanders once again across open country into devastating fire; and by the end of this third day under fire in the scorching sun the Argylls had 7 unwounded officers left, the Black Watch 6, and the Seaforths 5.

When the strenuous pursuit of the remaining Boer commandos came at last to an end, the 91st stayed on for a year or two, had another few years

in England, three years in Malta, and were in India when the German war broke out. Their service during 1914–18 was, as so often in the past, exacting but generally unrewarding. They were brought back to France for the Second Battle of Ypres, where they earned another battle honour and a special commendation from Sir John French. Thereafter they were in the forgotten theatre of Salonika, shoring up the weakening resistance of Serbs and Greeks, sometimes heavily engaged, but mostly contending with the climate and its attendant diseases, until the Bulgarian surrender on 30 September 1918 heralded the end of the war. By then they had only 237 all ranks on the ration strength; and half of them were employed on the line of communications.

It was the turn of the 93rd to be in the thick of things. They went through the whole mill of the fighting in France during 1914–18, winning golden

Officers of the 2nd Battalion at Aldershot, 1890

laurels at Le Cateau in their first engagement, and thereafter suffering all the disasters experienced by every regiment engaged in the futile Battle of Loos and on the Somme. They missed the worst of Passchendaele, but covered themselves with glory in the defence of Polygon Wood in the Third Battle of Ypres in September 1917. At Arras and in Polygon Wood they suffered the same sort of disaster as had overtaken them at New Orleans a hundred years before; and each time they showed the same resilience and, reinforced, returned to the battle with courage and morale unimpaired. There was more than an echo of Sir Colin Campbell's address to the 93rd at Balaklava in Sir Douglas Haig's immortal Order of the Day to his army at the crisis of the German offensive in March 1918 to 'fight on to the end' with their backs to the wall. The 93rd responded to Sir Douglas as they had to Sir Colin; and the armistice found them, still full of fight, close by Le Cateau where they had started their war.

Volumes could be, and indeed have been, written on the achievements of the five Territorial battalions and six Service battalions which the

Argylls put into the field between 1914 and 1918. Special mention should perhaps be made of the 8th Argyllshire Battalion, the most genuinely Highland of all, which distinguished itself even within the 51st Highland Division which the Germans listed as one of the most formidable fighting formations in the Allied Army. The most fitting short summary of the service of the rest is inscribed on the tablet in the moving shrine built into Edinburgh Castle as the Scottish National War Memorial:

'Ne Obliviscaris'
TO THE MEMORY
OF 431 OFFICERS AND
6,475 OTHER RANKS
OF THE REGIMENT
WHO GAVE THEIR LIVES
FOR KING AND COUNTRY
1914–1918

REGULARS
1ST BATTALION
91st (ARGYLLSHIRE) HIGHLANDERS
2nd BATTALION
93rd (SUTHERLAND) HIGHLANDERS

SPECIAL RESERVE
3rd and 4th BATTALIONS

TERRITORIALS
5th (RENFREWSHIRE)
6th (RENFREWSHIRE)
7th (STIRLINGSHIRE)
8th (ARGYLLSHIRE)
9th (DUMBARTONSHIRE)

SERVICE BATTALIONS
10th, 11th, 12th, 13th, 14th, 15th

'MONS'	'SOMME, 1916, '18'
'LE CATEAU'	'ARRAS, 1917, '18'
'MARNE, 1914–18'	'CAMBRAI, 1917, '18'
'YPRES, 1915, '17, '18'	'DOIRAN, 1917, '18'
'LOOS'	'GAZA'

'Sans Peur'
PRINCESS LOUISE'S ARGYLL AND
SUTHERLAND HIGHLANDERS

Some of the 8th Battalion in winter kit, Beaumont Hamel area, 1916. The Balmoral bonnet superseded the glengarry for working dress about this time and continued to be worn down to the 1960s

The Argyll and Sutherland Highlanders, 1919-1945

Like so many other great institutions, the British Army made a determined and prolonged effort after the war to recover a world which had perished for ever in 1914. The vast influx of civilian soldiers was demobilized as quickly as possible, and senior officers set themselves to re-constitute the old regular regiments. With the ranks filled up by young soldiers, mostly on short-term engagements, they resumed the rhythm of the Cardwell system. The 91st sailed for India to complete its interrupted tour of foreign service. The 93rd, shockingly depleted in numbers, re-formed in Scotland. But both at home and abroad they moved into a new world. Everywhere the fratricidal war of the Western Powers had released forces which were changing the whole political and social climate.

The 91st returned, not to the glamour of the British Raj, but to the khaki-clad monotony of barrack life and intensive training, punctuated by the distasteful business of quelling communal riots provoked by nationalist and revolutionary agitators. After four years of that they moved to Egypt, where things were soon even worse. They played a lot of games and played them very well. But almost immediately a mutiny of Egyptian troops in the Sudan involved them in bitter street fighting in Khartum and cost them 1 officer and 5 men killed, and 8 wounded. For the young soldiers it was their first serious fight, and they did very well. But the next four years in Cairo were enlivened only by the presentation of new Colours by Lord Lloyd. By 1930 they had completed twenty-two years of foreign service and were back in Edinburgh doing their share of Royal guards at Holyrood and Balmoral; and at Tidworth in 1935 they mounted their last parade in the old full dress. The scarlet coats and feathered bonnets vanished for ever, save for the rare appearances of officers in levée dress. The process of erosion which was to reduce the whole army to the drab discomfort of battle dress had begun.

The home service of the 93rd was equally dis-illusioning. It started with a spell of guard-mounting in Glasgow railway stations during the prolonged rail strike of 1919, which was followed by eighteen months of nerve-racking, unrewarding service against the Sinn Fein in Ireland. They had a respite then until 1927 in the Isle of Wight, where they too received new Colours from their Colonel-in-Chief before setting off on a highly nomadic tour of foreign service. They briefly re-visited the West Indies, had the odd distinction of being the only British unit ever to pass through the Panama Canal on their way to Hong Kong, and joined the international force which protected Shanghai's foreign communities when the old order in the Far East crumbled under the Japanese invasion of Manchuria. They recovered a faint flavour of the romance of nineteenth-century soldiering when they had to provide anti-pirate guards for ships plying up and down the Yangtze, and still more when they got to Rawalpindi in 1933 and were involved in the last of the frontier operations in North-West India which had so strongly coloured the military life of Kipling's world. In the two Mohmand campaigns, and on their old, 1895 hunting ground of Waziristan, they qualified both for the last issue of the India General Service Medal, and the first clasp of the new General Service Medal which replaced it.

For the last few years before the Second World War both battalions were involved in the hectic experimental efforts of the British Army to bring its organization and equipment up to date, as the public slowly awoke to the true facts of the international situation. Back at Tidworth the 91st were turned into a mechanized machine-gun battalion as part of an experimental mechanized brigade. It then dawned on higher authority that linked battalions constantly reinforcing each other must be trained and equipped identically; so the 93rd went through the same process at Secunderabad in southern India. Almost immediately, however, they were reconverted to ordinary infantry battalions; and this they were when the outbreak of war found the 91st busily engaged in hunting down Arab terrorists in Palestine, and the 93rd *en route* for Malaya as part of the 12th Indian Brigade.

Thanks to Hore-Belisha's last-minute doubling of the paper strength of the Territorial Army, the Argylls started the Second World War with the same number of battalions as in the First. But only eight in all saw active service overseas, and only five of those as infantry. The 5th and 6th (Renfrewshire) Battalions were retrained as anti-tank gunners; and the 9th (Dumbartonshire) became the 54th Light Anti-Aircraft Regiment. But they all, to the exasperated fury of the High Command, obstinately refused to be properly incorporated into the Royal Regiment of Artillery. The 5th and 6th became the 91st and 93rd Anti-Tank Regiment, Argyll and Sutherland Highlanders. They kept their Balmoral bonnets and Argyll insignia, their pipe bands, and a jealously guarded hoard of kilts for NCOs and pipers. They thus preserved the quality and traditions of battalions which already had a fine fighting record to live up to, and which would have been hard to create in a new *ad hoc* fortuitously gathered unit.

The war record of the 91st conformed quite remarkably to the pattern laid down in their previous history: more than a fair share of hardship and losses, inadequately rewarded by occasional spectacular successes. They hung on in Palestine, embittered and frustrated, until the apparent victory of Germany in Europe brought Italy into the war. Then they found themselves abruptly in the front line, when Wavell held the Egyptian frontier with two divisions against four Italian army corps; and they spearheaded the 90-mile advance which routed the Italian Army and captured Sidi Barrâni: an operation which, as Wavell had foretold, was 'one of the decisive

actions of the war'. They had a short, restful period guarding airfields, and were then plunged into the forlorn attempt to hold Crete as a bastion against the German sweep through the Balkans to the Mediterranean. Before they had even time to concentrate the battalion they were struck by the airborne assault to which the enemy had committed some 1,200 planes, themselves unsupported from the air and heavily outnumbered. The upshot of a short and gallant struggle was that only half the battalion – 312 out of the 655 who had landed – was brought out by the heroic self-sacrifice of the navy. It was a crippling blow.

Consequently, for two years the 91st were only on the fringe of great events in Ethiopia, Palestine and the Western Desert. Swollen by miscellaneous attachments, they formed a 'Beach Brick' – a special organization to control the landing of reinforcements and stores across the beaches – for the landings in Sicily and Italy. But only after the Sangro crossing did they find themselves back in the firing line as an infantry battalion for the crossing of the Rapido and the great Cassino battle. Thereafter, in the 8th Army's great drive

The Mons drum. Lost to the Germans at Le Cateau by the 93rd, it was generously restored to the regiment as a gesture of peace by the Germans after the War

The last parade in full dress – the Tidworth Tattoo, 1935

to the Gothic Line, they showed all the resilience of a great regiment, regaining, as one commander told them, 'a reputation for dash and tenacity which cannot be excelled'. To their pride, moreover, when the war ended, they were still 99 per cent Scots.

When the unexpected Japanese assault across the Siamese frontier caught the whole British defence system in Malaya on the wrong foot, the 93rd was almost the only unit which had been trained by a dynamic Commanding Officer, Ian Stewart, realistically in the jungle which the army authorities persistently regarded as 'impenetrable'. Against overwhelming enemy numbers well supported by armour, unchallenged in the air, and victorious at sea, the Argylls inevitably found themselves fighting a costly series of rearguard actions covering the withdrawal of the army to its last mainland stand along the Slim River. They were reduced by then to 3 officers and 90 men, though there were many small parties still at large in the jungle behind the enemy lines, the stories of whose prolonged heroism are too numerous to be told, and many more who left no survivors to tell their stories. When Captain Drummond Hay had brought up another hundred men who had discharged themselves, mostly unofficially, from office jobs in the rear, and when every man who could hobble had got out of hospital, they were able to form two companies and a headquarters group, in all 250 strong. They were joined by 200 marines rescued from the *Repulse*, and they went into their last great battle as the 'Plymouth Argylls'. As such, they were the last to cross to Singapore Island, marching in stately open order, their two surviving pipers in front playing 'A Hundred

Pipers' and 'Hielan' Laddie', with Drummer Hardy at the rear, alone, unhurried, and heedless of the shouts of sappers anxious to blow the necessary gaps in the causeway. As the Island battle reached its disastrous climax, Brigadier Stewart found himself isolated with the last survivors of the 93rd – 2 officers and 50 men – lying exhausted, black and greasy from fire-fighting. He had once promised them that he would never in battle say 'Go on', but always 'Come on'. Now, he said, he gave no order. He asked only: 'Will you come with me into this last battle?' Nobody answered, but all got to their feet. They advanced, in fact, into imprisonment; and in the long, heart-breaking years which followed there was no recorded case in the 93rd of loss of morale.

With the 91st virtually crippled and the 93rd annihilated, the burden of maintaining the great fighting tradition of the Argylls fell on the 7th and 8th Battalions. Conscious of this, they covered themselves with glory; both were in action in early days in France. The 7th is reputed to have seen more active service than any other British battalion; as part of the reconstituted 51st Highland Division they accompanied Montgomery to Alamein, fought their way through North Africa, Sicily and southern Italy, and then from Normandy to the Baltic. They suffered heavily in holding a precarious bridgehead across the minefield and anti-tank ditch at Sidi-Rezegh, where their Commanding Officer, Lorne Campbell, won his V.C.; and they were all but extinguished in a night fight with German paratroops at Gerbini airfield in Sicily. But they were still full of fight when they helped to clear the Reichswald, in February 1945, at the point of the bayonet. Apart from their Commanding Officer's V.C., they won sixty decorations for gallantry in the field. The pattern of the 8th Battalion's war was different, but no less distinguished. Half of them, led by Lorne Campbell, then their Second-in-Command, escaped from the encirclement of the original 51st Division at Saint-Valéry. Rebuilt on this foundation, they were back in the fighting with the 1st Army in Tunisia, where Major Jock Anderson won their V.C., rallying a wavering attack to carry Longstop Hill. Thereafter they too were in Sicily, and they fought their way up the length of Italy, winning on the way the even more remarkable total of ninety-eight decorations.

But perhaps the most convincing proof of the extent to which the Territorial battalions had inherited and imbibed the ancient traditions of the regiment was given by the most junior of the Hore-Belisha battalions, the 15th, when, on 28 May 1942, it was suddenly informed on a ceremonial parade by the Colonel of the Regiment that it had ceased to exist and was to be immediately reconstituted as the 93rd, to take over 'the name, the honours, and the traditions of that celebrated battalion'. In tribute to the Malayan tragedy the Chaplain said a prayer, the buglers sound the Last Post, and the pipers played the 'Flowers of the Forest'. But then they sounded Reveille as a defiant assertion that the old 93rd still lived, and marched off parade to 'Hielan' Laddie'.

It is not easy to understand how and why this unusually imaginative gesture by the War Office succeeded so brilliantly. The new 93rd had to wait for its baptism of fire until the great break-out from Monty's bridgehead by the 15th Scottish Division on 26 June 1944. In that two-day, five-mile advance, it was the 93rd who captured and held the two vital bridges over the River Odon. Thereafter they took part in every major assault of the campaign, ending up with a costly crossing of the Elbe only two days before VE Day. The most convincing tribute to their achievement is to be found in the foreword which the Colonel of the Regiment, Lieutenant-General Sir Gordon MacMillan wrote for the history of the reconstituted battalion:

'It was plain indeed for me to see during the time I had the honour to be their Divisional Commander that they were indeed the 93rd and not a new wartime unit with no background in history.

'There is little difficulty in seeing history repeating itself throughout this narrative.

'In 1813, 524 officers, NCOs and men of the 93rd fell before the fire of General Andrew Jackson's defenders of New Orleans, holding their ground because they had received no order to withdraw. In June 1944 the new 93rd, in its first action, stubbornly retained its position in the face of sustained German attacks when almost surrounded, refusing to accept an order to come back until its authenticity had been checked beyond doubt. Similar examples of tenacity were displayed by another 93rd in April 1917, at Arras, and at Polygon Wood in September the same year.'

General MacMillan had won his first M.C. and served as Adjutant in that 'other 93rd' in the First World War; and the reconstituted battalion could ask for no finer testimonial than this tribute from him.

The Latest Chapter

For the Regiment the most important consequence of victory was the final disappearance of the 93rd which had so often risen triumphant from its ashes. After a spell of comfortable garrison duty in Schleswig-Holstein, complicated only by refugee problems and occasional ticklish situations along the border of the Russian Zone, they went in 1947 into 'suspended animation'. Stirling Castle was to

Headquarters of the 8th Battalion moving up for the attack on Longstop Hill, 1943

house their traditions and impedimenta for some ten years until the 91st in turn receded and the 93rd took over. In practice this clumsy arrangement suited neither the Regiment nor the War Office. The 1st Battalion was charged by the Colonel with the duty of absorbing and embodying all the fine traditions of both its great progenitors; and this it most nobly did for the next twenty-four years. The fusion was happy and complete; and when the new battalion touched at Singapore in 1949 it still contained not only members of the reconstituted 93rd of 1944, but Major Slessor and nineteen men of the old battalion lost in Malaya.

By then the Argylls, reprieved by atomic bombs from the daunting prospect of driving the Japanese from their South-East Asia conquests, had already spent a trying time in Palestine, where Jewish terrorism had become a greater menace to the British Mandate than ever the Arabs had been. Partition made things worse; and they suffered a number of casualties in the thankless task of keeping the peace before the British at last pulled out. They then had two peaceful years, one in Colchester and one in Hong Kong, until, along

with the 1st Middlesex, who had shared with the 93rd the honours of the Battle of the Scarpe in 1917, they became the spearhead of a United Nations force, predominantly American, designated to halt the southerly advance of the Communist North Koreans.

They landed in Korea at the end of August 1950 and were plunged straight into action to help the Americans stem the first enemy onrush which had carried them to the Naktong River. The success of this operation enabled the Allies to mount an immediate counter-offensive; and the new Argylls then had the chance to show how completely they were entitled to rank with the men of Corunna, New Orleans, Balaklava, Polygon Wood and Gavrus. They were given as their objective a strongly held position known on the map as Hill 282, and after heavy fighting they carried it, only to find it completely dominated by a neighbouring higher hill, No. 388. Major Kenny Muir, the Second-in-Command, whose father had commanded the 91st and who had himself briefly commanded the 93rd before their disbandment, took up a party of stretcher-bearers to the hard-pressed leading companies and found himself instead reorganizing what had become a desperate defence. It crumbled completely when the air strike he called for on 388 heavily machine-gunned his own clearly marked positions instead, and then drenched them with napalm bombs. Major Muir nevertheless rallied the surviving 5 officers and 35 men and reoccupied the still burning hill. When the last of the rifle ammunition ran out, he himself was still firing a two-inch mortar and shouting, 'The Gooks [North Koreans] will never get the Argylls off this hill.' Then he too was killed, having by his gallantry added one more to the regiment's long list of V.C.s.

The Battalion had lost one company, killed almost to a man, and many more wounded. But reinforcements were available, and with characteristic resilience it was back in the forefront of the advance which was halted and turned back by the intervention of Chinese 'volunteers'. During a bleak winter campaign reminiscent of the Crimea they again hit the headlines when they went to the rescue of a hard-pressed American artillery battalion which was running out of rifle ammunition. Their successful action brought them a generous letter of thanks from the American Divisional Commander, expressing admiration for their 'discipline, coolness, and workmanship' under fire; and there is no doubt that when they left for a well-earned eighteen months' rest in Hong Kong their reputation stood very high indeed throughout the Allied Army.

Their doings had also greatly caught the imagination of the public at home, and they returned to a tumultuous welcome in their native land such as has seldom been seen. From Her Majesty the Queen, who had graciously consented to continue as their Colonel-in-Chief on her accession, there was a special congratulatory message awaiting them when they had marched, bands playing, through the thronged streets of Glasgow to a civic reception by the Lord Provost amidst cheering so wild that one tough old docker was heard to remark that he had seen many homecomings, but that this was one he would 'never forget'. Their welcome in Edinburgh was, if anything, even more tumultuous, with Princes Street closed to traffic and every pavement, window, balcony and roof-top jammed with cheering crowds. There was a smaller but no less enthusiastic reception at their own home in Stirling;

and, finally, the Provost, bailies and remanent councillors granted them 'the freedom of entry into the Burgh of Dunoon on ceremonial occasions with bayonets fixed, drums beating, and colours flying'. It was a heart-warming and thoroughly well-deserved recognition of 150 years of selfless courage and devotion to duty.

That was in the autumn of 1952; and the Argylls were not to find themselves in the limelight again for fifteen years. But those years were far from inactive. They had scarcely begun the round of intensive training punctuated by Scottish ceremonial duties when they were sent at short notice to British Guiana. There the old 93rd Dublin recipe of 'kind and steady, yet decided conduct' transformed a potentially explosive situation into a pleasant year of social and sporting activity. They then had two short spells at home, separated by eighteen months' garrison duty in Berlin, before superintending the unpleasant business of evacuating Port Said in 1956. In the next ten years they had a relatively quiet time at home or in Germany, though with two instructive interruptions: in Cyprus, where the same old recipe gained them great praise for 'steadiness and calmness under great provocation'; and briefly in Borneo. The total effect of these fifteen active years was that, when they arrived in Aden in June 1967, there was no British battalion with more direct experience of counter-insurgency tactics.

Even four years later, controversy still rages over the events surrounding the reoccupation, on 3 July 1967, of the town of Crater, the heart of Aden and the active source of all the subversive

The 93rd riding up to the start line for the assault on the Siegfried Line, 28 February 1945

A command vehicle of the Argyll and Sutherland High-landers in the Crater district of Aden. At the wheel is Lt. Col. Colin Mitchell, well known to the British public as 'Mad Mitch'. Note the cloth shoulder title slipped over Mitchell's shoulder-strap, bearing rank insignia and the tally 'A & SH'; the canisters of CS irritant gas clipped to the bulkhead of the Land Rover; the self-loading rifles carried by the two Jocks in the rear of the vehicle; and, just visible at low left, the 9 mm Sterling sub-machine gun carried by the obscured soldier in the back. Note the extra bandolier worn by the left-hand rifleman (Daily Express)

terrorism which was bedevilling the life of the whole Protectorate. The historian can only record the known facts and leave them to speak for themselves. The Argylls moved into Crater with the maximum panache, led by the Pipe-Major, and dealt very firmly with all active opposition. For five months thereafter they completely dominated the town from well-armed observation posts on the roofs of the highest buildings which subdued, and ultimately eliminated, all enemy sniping; and when the Protectorate was finally abandoned and they returned to Plymouth, every officer and man was proud of a good job well done. It had cost them 5 killed and 25 wounded, more casualties than had been sustained in eleven years in Suez, Cyprus and Borneo put together.

Inevitably the whole operation had been given full publicity. Journalists and television cameras were everywhere, and everyone in the regiment had to learn the techniques of public relations. The general principle laid down by Lieutenant-Colonel Mitchell was to tell the news hawks everything and trust them not to mention what they were asked to keep quiet – trust, be it said, which was never once misplaced. It remains a mystery, not only to all closely associated with the Argylls but to the public at large, why this wholly successful operation earned the bitter condemnation of the local High Command. Possibly the skilful publicity of an exceptionally self-confident, outspoken, and perhaps even excessively self-assured Commanding Officer, and the reactions of the Jocks, who almost all showed themselves to be TV 'naturals', gave offense. Stories of Argyll brutality may certainly be dismissed as revolutionary moonshine. Equally certainly the overwhelming weight of British public opinion shared the resentment of the Argylls themselves as the slur cast on them when their Commanding Officer was the only one to be pointedly excluded from the list of those awarded the D.S.O. for the service their units had rendered in the Aden crisis. Rightly or wrongly, it was judged to be a mean and vindictive gesture. But time brings its revenges, and it undoubtedly helped not only to sweep Colonel Mitchell into Parliament, but to swell to a million, the signatures collected to help the regiment in its last desperate battle for survival, this time against the Ministry of Defence. General Freddie Graham, who had succeeded Sir Gordon MacMillan as Colonel of the Regiment, rigidly and rightly refused the compromise of amalgamation. Even a change of government and the election of Mitchell could only force a grudging concession from the War Department, whereby the Argylls were permitted to survive in the attenuated form of an independent company.

Balaklava Company, formally inaugurated at Stirling Castle by Her Majesty the Queen on 20 January 1971, showed itself fully capable of shouldering the enormous burden of 150 years of glorious regimental history. By the end of that first summer it was already reliably reported to have transformed in a most lively manner the social, sporting, and even the military life of the garrison of Gibraltar. In 1972 the joyful news was received that the Regiment was to be revived; and Balaklava Company returned to Edinburgh to become the nucleus of the rebuilt 1st Battalion.

Recruits flowed in; trained soldiers returned from the regiments to which they had been attached since 1970; and by the spring of 1972 the battalion was once again alive and training for an active role, this time in Ulster.

The Argylls since that date have carried out a number of unaccompanied four or six month operational tours as well as a full two year tour in that troubled Province. They have also served twice in Germany as a mechanised battalion, in Catterick, Hong Kong – where they helped control attempted

Cruachan and the Pipes and Drums of the 1st Battalion

illegal immigration from across the Chinese border, Cyprus, Edinburgh, Colchester, the Falklands Islands, Shorncliffe and most recently Redford Barracks in Edinburgh.

Her Majesty The Queen, as Colonel-in-Chief, has visited the 1st Battalion in Catterick (1978), Edinburgh (1984) and Shorncliffe (1994) and presented new colours to the 1st Battalion in Edinburgh in 1973 and 1996. Her Majesty also presented new Colours to 3rd/ 51st Highland Volunteers, at Stirling in 1986. In 1996 this unit was renamed the 7th/ 8th Battalion of the Argyll and Sutherland Highlanders, and continues the direct linkage between regular and territorial army battalions of the regiment.

In 1972 Maj.Gen. Freddie Graham retired as Colonel of the Regiment and was succeeded by Brig. A C S Boswell – later Lt.Gen. Sir Alexander Boswell – who subsequently handed over to Maj.Gen. Palmer, (later Gen. Sir Patrick Palmer) in 1982. Maj.Gen. D P Thomson then took over as Colonel of the Regiment in 1992.

What lies ahead? The world of the British Army has shrunk since the days of the Empire but despite a reduction in overseas garrisons there are still tremendous opportunities for members of the Battalion to serve and train in such diverse locations as Canada, Kenya, New Zealand, Australia, Brunei, Poland, Russia, Bosnia, Nepal, Zimbabwe, Falkland Islands, South Africa and Sweden.

The Plates

A1 Officer, Battalion Company, 93rd Highlanders, 1801

This is the uniform in which the Sutherland Highlanders were first raised. The so-called 'little kilt' had recently replaced the old single garment, the belted plaid, but the decorative plaid worn over the left shoulder as a vestigial remnant of the old garment had not yet been sanctioned. The jacket is buttoned to the neck, as for action or field training. For more formal occasions the top two buttons would be undone and buttoned back to form two yellow-faced lapels. This facing ran down to the bottom of the coat on both sides. For full, or ball dress the facings would be completely buttoned back and hooked together down the middle to make a plastron of yellow, laced with silver. The silver epaulettes were to be replaced by gold throughout the Highland Brigade in 1804.

A2 Private, Battalion Company, 93rd Highlanders, 1805

This man shows both the distinguishing marks of the Battalion Companies: the red and white hackle in the bonnet and the tufts of lamb's wool on the shoulders instead of wings. This is how he first went into action at the Cape, with galoshes over his pewter-buckled shoes and black gaiters as worn by all non-commissioned ranks. The coat is single-breasted and the cross-belt buckle a different shape from the officer's and of bronze picked out with brass, instead of silver and gilt; and his buttons are pewter instead of silver. But, like his officer, he does not turn down the hose

over his garters – a custom unique to the 93rd. The musket is the standard flint-lock of the period to which, before charging, he would affix a triangular bayonet.

A3 Captain, 91st Argyllshire Highlanders, 1808

This represents the uniform worn by officers of the 91st during the first fifteen years of the regiment's existence, before it lost its Highland status and accoutrements altogether. The 91st always conformed much more strictly to the Dress Regulations for His Majesty's Highland Regiments than did the 93rd. They always wore, for example, a white edging of false collar round the inside of the black stock. The plain, steel-hilted broadsword, without regimental insignia, was the standard pattern for the Highland Brigade. They turned their hose down over their garters, and they wore no fox-tails on their feathered bonnets. The sporran, also, conformed exactly to the standard pattern: so much so, that on one occasion, when Lochnell had ordered too many, he was able to sell off the surplus to another regiment. The tartan is that described by Lochnell in his letter to the Duke of Argyll – the dark green Campbell, with the black line, which was in fact almost indistinguishable from the Sutherland. The gorget, too, is worn, correctly, suspended from a yellow ribbon round the neck, and not hung, as in the 93rd, from two small gold buttons.

An Argyll patrol pauses during an operation in the back-country of Aden. A 2nd Lieutenant passes messages to a radio operator using the A. 41 back-pack radio set; this equipment has a range of about five miles. The troops are armed with the 7·62mm high-velocity SLR, a semi-automatic weapon with a twenty-round magazine. The Jock on the right carries a 200-round belt of 7·62mm ammunition for the squad's General Purpose Machine Gun (GPMG). The large silver-finish cap badges on the glengarries show clearly (Daily Express)

This particular officer is wearing the Peninsular Medal, and may be presumed to have recently arrived back in Scotland from Corunna.

B1 Officer, Battalion Company, 93rd Highlanders, 1834

The uniform has not changed in essentials since 1800, save for the addition of the half plaid which, with its rosette on the shoulder, had become an altogether more elaborate piece of decoration than it was in the Peninsular period. The two elaborately embroidered nine-inch coat tails – known as skirts – were very soon to be shortened to similarly embroidered semicircular skirts, and two more were added in front, on either side of the sporran; and in this form the officer's coat was to survive as part of full, or levée, dress until 1939.

B2 Field Officer, 91st Argyllshire Highlanders, 1808

At Christmas, 1804, full Highland dress was restored to the 91st in place of the detested Cape uniform (see p. 13). But Dress Regulations for Highland regiments had changed since 1795. Officers wore full Highland dress for all duties, but off duty changed to white breeches and Hessian boots. Field and staff officers wore breeches and half-boots at all times, and carried a sabre instead of the broadsword. The 93rd, always wayward in such matters, appear to have ignored these regulations. The 91st were more conformist, and this lieutenant-colonel is correct in every particular. He retains his 91st coat and bonnet; and the tartan silk waist and shoulder sashes, with the narrow crimson stripe over the shoulder, were standard wear for all Highland field officers. He also wears the recently introduced half-plaid, slung from the left shoulder and hitched to the belt at the back, under the coat.

B3 Sergeant, Grenadier Company, 93rd Highlanders, 1814

For the New Orleans campaign, the 93rd were deprived of their kilts and put into trews. The feathered bonnet was also left at home, leaving only the Kilmarnock cocked bonnet which was its base. In the Highlands this was normally worn uncocked, that is without any stiffening inside, so that it lay flat on the top of the head; and it was known as the 'Humble' bonnet. The marks which

An Argyll road-block during a stop-and-search operation in Aden. A GPMG with the ammunition belt housed in a side-box is trained to give cover while troops with SLRs at the ready search a Volkswagen for arms or explosives. The Jocks are wearing the standard 58 Pattern webbing equipment. Two ammunition pouches are worn on each side of the belt buckle, the left-hand pouch having an integral sheath for the bayonet. With Tropical Service Dress two canteens are carried, one on each hip. Two large rear pouches carry mess-tins, rations, and personal effects. When worn, the large pouch for the gas-mask is slung centrally on the front of the belt (Daily Express)

distinguish this sergeant as belonging to the Grenadier Company are the wings which replace the lamb's-wool tufts on his shoulders and the white 'tourie' on top of the bonnet, recalling the white hackle which he would normally wear on his feathered bonnet. Battalion Companies wore a red tourie and the Light Company a dark green one.

C1 Corporal, Grenadier Company, 93rd Highlanders, 1838

Here again nothing essential has changed. But the whole impression has acquired a more aggressive panache. The bonnet is an inch higher and the fox-tails on it are longer. This was, of course, the great period for the elaboration of uniforms in all European armies. But it is worth noting that the taller bonnet had its practical value in action: it added an apparent foot to the height of a line of charging Highland soldiers as they emerged from the smoke and dust of a battlefield and made them look even more formidable than they already were.

C2 Private, 91st Argyllshire Regiment, 1846

This picture is designed to illustrate the rage and frustration felt by the large body of officers and men of Scottish origin still serving in the regiment at being excluded from the Highland Brigade and reduced to the appearance and status of an ordinary British line regiment. Only the '91' on their chacos and the designation of 'Argyllshire' survived to remind them of their origins.

C3 Piper, 93rd Highlanders, 1853

This was the uniform in which the pipers were to lead the 93rd in their epic period, up the heights of the Alma, and to the relief of Lucknow. It was aggressively Sutherland, with its full plaid and the green doublet skirted on the same pattern as that of the officers. Their hose, however, differed from the regimental pattern; and they had accepted the convention of turning down their hose-tops over the garter, which the rest of the regiment was still to defy for some time to come.

D1 Officer, Light Company, 93rd Highlanders, 1853

This, in terms of uniform, represents the full flowering of the old 93rd. This was the uniform of the 'Thin Red Line' and the storming of the Sikandarbargh Gate. There are no great changes to note, save that the kilt has become a little longer, the design of the cross-belt buckle has been altered, and, for the first time, the *sgean dubh* is shown tucked into the hose below the right knee. His status as a Light Company officer is shown by the tall green hackle and the gold lace wings in place of epaulettes. The advent of the Minié rifle was soon to make Light Companies in infantry battalions redundant. But he is ahead of his time in wearing a moustache, since they did not become compulsory for British officers until 1856.

D2 Bandboy, 93rd Highlanders, 1856

This is the uniform of both drummers and band-boys at the period of the Crimean and Mutiny campaigns, and as far as the detail of accoutrements go, the picture is self-explanatory. This young man's Crimean medal with its three clasps suggests that he has only recently graduated to his oboe and had taken part as a drummer in the battles of the Alma and Balaklava. So long as troops fought in close order drummers had a vital part to play in the thick of the battle, beating time and sounding various calls. An American observer records a vivid memory of a drummer boy at New Orleans in 1815, clinging to the branch of a tree

The Royal Salute at the Inauguration of the Balaklava Company by H.M. The Queen at Stirling Castle on 8th January 1970

and cheering wildly as the 93rd moved up in line to its last, disastrous position; and Kipling's story of *The Drums of the Fore and Aft* shows that things had not much changed at the end of the century. One might also record that a drummer of the 93rd was the last man across the causeway on to Singapore Island in 1942.

D3 Officer, 91st Highlanders, 1857

The beginnings of the rehabilitation of the 91st as a Highland regiment. This officer is still denied his tartan and bonnet, but the unsightly English chaco is at least decorated with a specifically Scottish badge, and the red and white tourie commemorates the hackle he would have worn as a Battalion Company officer in his feathered bonnet.

E1 Officer, Grenadier Company, 93rd Highlanders, 1857

This is the fighting uniform of the Mutiny campaign. Before going into action this officer is buttoning a light dust-coat over his scarlet, over which he has already put on a second belt carrying a holstered revolver. He also wears under his feathered bonnet a stiffened screen to protect the back of his neck against the sun. For the rest the uniform is standard; and the white hackle denotes his company.

E2 Ensign, 93rd Highlanders, 1857

This officer is depicted as he might have been seen leading the assaults on the Sikandarbargh Gate and the Shah Najaf. Except at moments of great emergency the Colours were carried cased to save them from wear and damage. But on the evening of this operation they were in fact uncased and flown from the tower of the Shah Najaf to show the hard-pressed defenders of the Lucknow Residency that relief was close at hand.

E3 Lieutenant, 8th Argyll Rifle Volunteers, 1866
This is a good example of the type of officer who responded to the 1859 call for Rifle Volunteers. He wears the green jacket of a rifleman and has a bugle on his belt-plate; but the rest of his uniform, with the full, ceremonial plaid brought forward over the left shoulder, is a defiant assertion of the deep-rooted Argyllshire loyalties which persisted, and still persist, in the famous 8th Argyllshire Battalion of the Argyll and Sutherland Highlanders. He wears, however, the controversial Breadalbane tartan in which the 91st were rehabilitated in the Highland Brigade in 1864. This imposition of an east coast tartan on a specifically west coast regiment was particularly resented by the Volunteers.

F1 Sergeant, 91st Highlanders, 1874
The uniform of the restored 91st as it would be worn on field manœuvres or in action, with the trews tucked into black gaiters. The coat has acquired three shortened tails behind instead of the traditional two. The ridiculous kepi – in effect a shortened chaco with dicing added round the base – persisted until the restoration of the kilt. But they were allowed on fatigue and off parade to wear the glengarry, here shown carried under the straps of the pack.

F2 Field Officer, Argyll and Sutherland Highlanders, 1882
Though the amalgamated regiment after 1881 was recruited almost entirely from south-west Scotland, in matters of dress the customs of the old 93rd, which had never lost its Highland identity, prevailed. The tartan was theirs, as were the bonnet, with its six fox-tails, and the badger sporran with its six white tassels. This officer, though he is dressed only for a semi-formal occasion and is not wearing kilt and sporran, sufficiently illustrates this point.

F3 Sergeant, Argyll and Sutherland Highlanders, 1882
This picture illustrates the white shell jacket which was worn for fatigues and most drill parades from the amalgamation until the Boer War. It also shows the kilt and badger sporran inherited from the old 93rd, but the glengarry badge emphasizes the fusion of the two regiments and the emergence of the new one as 'Princess Louise's Own'.

G1 Officer, Undress, Argyll and Sutherland Highlanders, 1892
The blue patrol coat was introduced as a compromise between mufti and drill order or mess dress as needed on more formal occasions: and it proved itself so useful that its use has continued and expanded to the present day. This officer is probably the orderly officer of the day waiting until it is time to go round turning out the guards. If he were merely dawdling before going over to the ante-room for a drink before dinner he would not be wearing gloves. In the course of time the frogs on this jacket would disappear and brass buttons would appear down the front and on the cuffs. Patent leather dress wellington boots would also replace these clumsy laced ones.

G2 Private, Volunteer Battalion, Argyll and Sutherland Highlanders, 1902
This uniform represents an interim period before, under the impact of Haldane's 1908 reforms, all such battalions became Territorial battalions of the parent regiment and thenceforward conformed in all particulars of dress to the regimental customs. It is, however, an interesting illustration of what the Kilmarnock bonnet looked like when uncocked – that is with the internal stiffening removed.

G3 Private, Highland Division, 1940
The standard khaki battle-dress, including khaki Balmoral bonnet, as worn by the Argylls during the early days of Wavell's campaign in the Western Desert. On his left arm this private wears the distinctive red-and-white chequered flash of the Argylls, beneath which is the red-and-blue badge of the Highland Division. All equipment is the standard khaki webbing issue.

Balaklava Company in Gibraltar, 1971; field training just below the summit of the Rock

H1 Piper, Argyll and Sutherland Highlanders, No. 1 Dress, 1960

Between the world wars all regiments were engaged on a determined rearguard battle to restore and preserve their pre-1914 dress and customs, and their peculiar tribal customs the Highland Brigade from such hideous innovations as the khaki plus-fours of English service dress in the 1930s. After 1945, however, there was an attempt, in the name of 'economy', to impose uniformity in such matters as cap badges on the whole Highland Brigade. In 1960, in the face of universal resentment, the attempt was abandoned: and the last three plates represent the limited degree of freedom and idiosyncrasy finally allowed to the Argylls. Though shorn of some of the more flamboyant accessories of his nineteenth-century predecessors, this piper fairly represents their tradition. The picture speaks for itself and needs no further comment.

H2 Officer, Service Dress, Argyll and Sutherland Highlanders, 1960

As can be seen, though the scarlet coat has given way to khaki and the Sam Browne has replaced the old cross-belts and crimson sash, much of the old glory has survived. The Kilmarnock bonnet had a short life, since the Argylls soon obstinately reverted to the old glengarry, which they were still wearing in Aden in 1969. Officers still wear the panel on the kilt which was added to give it weight at the request, so tradition has it, of the Princess Louise after an embarrassingly revealing inspection of her regiment in a high wind towards the end of the last century.

H3 Sergeant, Argyll and Sutherland Highlanders, 1965

A final example of the usefulness of blue patrol. An orderly sergeant going about his business, easily identifiable as being on duty, but not formally on parade.